The *foundation* of success:
Direction, balance, belief.

The *definition* of success:
"Success is
the progressive realization
of predetermined, worthwhile goals,
stabilized with balance
and purified by belief."

SUCCESS!

THE GLENN BLAND METHOD

LIVING BOOKS
Tyndale House Publishers, Inc.
Wheaton, Illinois

This book is dedicated to the men who have had
the greatest influence on my life:

Billie Snell—*for his encouragement*
Joe Schuhardt—*for caring about me*
Jack Crawley—*for teaching me to win*
Melvin Reimer—*for his instruction*
Colonel Robert B. Thieme, Jr.—*for directing me to the truth*
Charles Baker—*for believing in me*
And to all of my colleagues with Coaches Insurance
Associates of America who believe in our philosophy.

Living Books is a registered trademark
of Tyndale House Publishers, Inc.

All Scriptures in this book
are from *The Living Bible, Paraphrased,*
unless otherwise indicated.

Living Books® edition

Library of Congress Catalog Card Number 74-21969
ISBN 0-8423-6689-X

14   15   16   92   91

Contents

Foreword

When I first met Glenn Bland five years ago, he told me of his ambitious plan to build "from scratch" one of America's largest and most successful life insurance sales organizations. Five years ago it was only a dream, but today it is a reality.

To my knowledge, the phenomenal success story of Glenn Bland and Coaches Insurance Associates of America is unparalleled in the history of the life insurance industry. His company produces more sales each year than many life insurance companies which have been in business for over half a century.

Why is Bland so successful? Because he understands and applies universal success principles most people never know about. He knows how to establish far-reaching goals and how to plan for their attainment. His world is an "action world"—a place where he makes good things happen, benefiting all mankind.

In this dynamic book you will have the opportunity to discover these secrets of personal success. You, too, can realize your dreams by learning to apply his methods to your life. The book was written from personal experience by this man who has "done it" and knows what he is talking about. Any individual who truly wants to succeed can do so by committing himself to following the Bland Method.

The author believes in building people, and has devoted much of his life to doing so. He wrote this book to direct men and women to a happy and prosperous life and to help others free themselves from the chains of ineptness and mediocrity, becoming the successful persons God intended them to be.

Regardless of who you are, or what your vocation, this book will help you find a better life if you will read it and believe!

Charles A. Baker
Senior Vice President
Lincoln American
Life Insurance Company

Part 1

How to Have a Happy and Successful Life

1

There Is a Way

If I were to draw a line and tell you that simply stepping over it would change your life for the better, would you take that step?

Certainly you would. And if you knew that taking that step would guarantee inner peace, riches, enlightenment, and physical well-being, you would not hesitate a second.

You will have an opportunity to take that step—right into a life of happiness and success—as you continue through this book.

Stepping across the line *does* work. Stepping across the line definitely led me to a life of happiness and success. I have shared my experience with close friends and business associates and with others I scarcely knew. In every instance, where the line was never recrossed, fantastic results have been achieved.

I have seen derelicts changed into decent people. Debt-ridden individuals into financial successes. Misguided souls into persons who possess the wisdom of the ages. Mentally and physically ill weaklings into healthy and productive citizens.

I have seen these miracles happen right before my

.eyes and they will happen again and again to those who follow the teachings of this book.

Before crossing this line, a young man in Houston was out of work, beset by ulcers and harried by obligations. Today, he is the leading salesman with his company.

In Lubbock, Texas, another young man was unhappy and rapidly losing ground in his work. After he crossed the line, he soon became one of the city's outstanding businessmen.

In Memphis, Tennessee, a man had literally failed at every undertaking, until he stepped across the line and adopted the principles outlined in this book. Today he is a business and financial success.

The secret that is the heart of these teachings will be presented herein. If you will let this book serve as a guiding light to direct you to follow its path to a life of happiness and success, then my efforts will have been worthwhile.

The Discovery of a New Life

But, first, let me tell you how this book came into being. Years of thought and study, months, weeks, days and hours of planning preceded the development of what I call the Bland Method of Goal Setting and Planning.

The development of this method was not an easy task. It demanded unwavering faith, unrelenting persistence, and the courage to act no matter what obstacles seemed to lie around every corner.

The principles in my method are not unique. They have been responsible for the making of kings, the building of empires, and the creation of vast fortunes. On the other hand, these principles have never stolen serenity from the lives of those who have used them.

Having discovered this secret and having applied it in my own life, I want now to share it with just as many people as possible.

My method of goal setting and planning had its beginning many years ago when I first became success conscious.

My fondest dreams involved happiness and success. I searched for the wisdom and the truth that could lead me to realizing those dreams.

I made a giant step toward success while browsing through a book shop in San Antonio's International Airport. I was attracted by a colorful blue and yellow cover and an appealing title. The book? *Think and Grow Rich,* by a man I had not heard of before named Napoleon Hill.

To help pass the time until my plane was due to leave, I bought the book and began to skim its pages.

As I read, I found something happening to me.

At that particular time in my life, I was doing my work well, but only because it was something that I had to do and not something I wanted to do. I was drifting. I had no real direction, no goals, no plans.

Because I *was* drifting, others dictated to me. I didn't understand the one basic principle, "Men who have goals and plans dictate to others, while men who have no goals or plans are dictated to."

As I read, the above principle revealed by Mr. Hill became increasingly important to me. I said to myself, "He has found the key that can unlock the door to happiness and success in my life. This is what I've been looking for!"

I read on and on and found myself in even greater agreement with the things Napoleon Hill stands for.

Almost before I realized it, I was in the living room

of my home, 200 miles from San Antonio, finishing the last pages of this fantastic book.

I hardly recall the flight from San Antonio to Waco. Time had flown by because on that evening my life was changed. I had become "success conscious" and an entire new world of meaning and opportunity had been opened for me.

Becoming aware of this new world is experienced by everyone who achieves success at some point in time.

"Success consciousness" is the place where all achievement begins. It's a time in your life when you first realize that there is a happy and successful way to live. At that time you suddenly know you can change your life for the better. You decide to change it and then you follow through and attain your desires.

Having become "success conscious" you develop a hunger for wisdom and truth and you begin to search for everything that you can read or hear to satisfy that hunger.

I have read many books, spent many hours listening to records and tapes with only one goal—to program my mind for happiness and success.

As I studied and accumulated wisdom, I hit upon a basic truth. It struck me like a bolt from the blue:

"Techniques and methods change, but principles never do!"

I knew exactly, at that moment, where to find the information that I had been searching for. The principles had never changed; everything you and I need to know about happiness and success is contained within the binding of one book—the Holy Bible.

There was no reason to search further or elsewhere because within the Bible's covers you find the distilled wisdom of the ages.

The Bible's principles, which have withstood all the tests of recorded time, generated all of the other books and records and tapes which had proved so helpful to me.

Within the Bible you will find the answer to all of life's opportunities and problems. It contains all of the principles found in every other book ever written about success and happiness. From the wellspring of the Creator, stimulating wisdom will never run dry. As we grow, our understanding grows, and more and more of the wisdom of the ages is opened to us. We are limited in our understanding only by our willingness to abide by the principles and to grow.

"I, Wisdom, give good advice and common sense. Because of my strength, kings reign in power. I show the judges who is right and who is wrong. Rulers rule well with my help. I love all who love me. Those who search for me shall surely find me. Unending riches, honor, justice and righteousness are mine to distribute. My gifts are better than the purest gold or sterling silver! My paths are those of justice and right. Those who love and follow me are indeed wealthy. I fill their treasuries. The Lord formed me in the beginning, before he created anything else. From ages past, I am. I existed before the earth began. I lived before the oceans were created, before the springs bubbled forth their waters onto the earth; before the mountains and the hills were made. Yes, I was born before God made the earth and fields, and high plateaus" (Proverbs 8:14-26).

Without question, "Techniques and methods change, but principles never do." They have existed in eternity past and will exist in eternity future. The principles for achieving happiness and success in your life today are the same principles that King Solomon used to create his vast fortune in 966 B.C.

This planet, called Earth, didn't just happen! It was created by an infinitely intelligent Being beyond our human understanding and this Creator established certain natural laws that put order into all things. If you plan your life to function within the boundaries of these natural laws, you can achieve happiness and success. If you live outside these natural laws, you will never enjoy the inner peace, riches, enlightenment, and physical well-being for which you are searching. It is as amazing and simple as that.

You may avoid the laws of man, but there are greater laws that cannot be broken. The Creator is the source of every natural law leading to happiness and success. He wants to share this wisdom with each of us and has outlined his plan for the ages in an inspired book, the Holy Bible.

Mankind faces great problems today because people have become so self-sufficient that they sometimes forget there is a God. They forget that there is an omnipresent power that is bigger and more powerful than you and I! God created everything that exists and he can certainly create something of such relative insignificance as happiness and success for a man if that man will play the game according to the rules.

W. E. Gladstone said, "I have known ninety-five of the world's great men in my time, and of these, eighty-seven were followers of the Bible. The Bible is stamped with a Speciality of Origin, and an immeasureable distance separates it from all competitors."

Napoleon Bonaparte said, "The Bible is no mere book, but a Living Creature, with a power that conquers all who oppose it."

Yes, "The Bible is no mere book," for through its message and from the other outstanding material you will be exposed to, the secret of happiness and success will leap from the written page and become a reality in your life. You will be asked to do only one thing as these principles are unfolded for you—*believe!*

You Must Take The "Can't" Out of Your Life

History reveals that there have always been those individuals who spend their lives in a negative world where "can't" is the most frequently used word in their vocabulary. Had such great men as Thomas Edison listened to the so-called experts of their day, our civilization would probably be regressing instead of progressing.

Here's proof. The following statements are taken from official documents, newspapers and magazines widely read during their day. Listen to what the "authorities" had to say:

    1840—"Anyone traveling at the speed of thirty miles per hour would surely suffocate."

    1878—"Electric lights are unworthy of serious attention."

    1901—"No possible combination can be united into a practical machine by which men shall fly."

    1926—(from a scientist) "This foolish idea of shooting at the moon is basically impossible."

    1930—(another scientist) "To harness the energy locked up in matter is impossible."

There have always been those who said, "It can't be done." Yes, even the experts can be wrong. But the real tragedy is that 99 percent of the people believed them.

We can be thankful that nonconformists, such as the Wright Brothers and Edison, did not accept what the so-called authorities said.

You can be sure of one thing—people who made

statements such as those quoted did not understand one of the most important and basic natural laws of the universe: "Anything you can think of and believe in, you can achieve!"

The mind of man can conceive many things, but believing them is something else. You might conceive the idea of earning one million dollars next year, but without *genuine belief* in your heart that it can be done, it will never become reality. Believing is the key! It is the basic ingredient of the happy and successful life.

Jesus made the same point in the following manner, "If you can believe, all things are possible to him that believes." Jesus did not eliminate anything. He said, "All things!" Why would Jesus make such a statement if it were not so? He understood the natural laws of the universe—he knew that the "Law of Belief" is just as certain as that day follows night. He used the power of belief to heal the sick, to change water into wine, and he said that if a man could develop his belief enough, he could even move mountains.

Belief is a powerful force and when properly used it can move man to accomplish great things! Our Creator gave us the choice of living in two worlds: positive or negative. A world where you "can" accomplish your lifetime dreams or a world where you "can't" do anything because of a million trivial excuses that hold you back. Quit thinking about all of the reasons why you "can't" do something and think of all the reasons why you "can." Decide now that you are going to be a member of that select group of successful people who live in a positive world—it is just too difficult to live any other way. Take the "can't" out of your life by *believing!*

The Essence of the Creator

Mankind has always been aware of God's creative force within our universe. The evidence of this great force is all around us. It is found in the birth of an infant, in the roar of a mighty ocean wave, in the unparalleled beauty of a flower, in your innermost feelings for a little child and in the magnificent design of a single snowflake. The evidence surrounds us but it is so commonplace that we take it for granted.

Each of us has the opportunity to use this creative force in our life to accomplish our goals, but few do so. This creative force has been given to us free—it costs nothing and to receive its full power we must only believe. As human beings, imperfect by nature, we place little value on things that we do not pay for. We value homes, automobiles, boats, television sets and, at the same time, place little or no value on the things in life that are free—our bodies, minds, families, friends, good health, love and the natural laws of the universe.

The truth is that the material things that we value highly are really very cheap and can be replaced. Your home can be destroyed by fire and it can be rebuilt. A man can lose his fortune and then replace it several times over. But when the things that are given to us free are lost—they are gone forever.

The statement, "The best things in life are free," is true. They are available for the taking. They are the things that are responsible for putting happiness into your life. To take advantage of the natural laws of the universe, to guide us to a life of happiness and success, we must understand the essence of the Creator, who governs all life and creation.

Sovereign: The Creator is the ruler of all things.

Righteous: It is impossible for the Creator to be wrong; he is perfect in every way.

Just: The Creator knows everything, all sides of every situation—therefore, it is impossible for him to be unfair.

Loving: The Creator gives perfect affection—a love beyond human love and understanding.

Eternal: The Creator has always existed, is very much alive today, and will always exist—he is everlasting.

Omniscient: The Creator knows everything—all ideas come from his infinite mind.

Omnipotent: The Creator has the power to do anything—he is all-powerful and able.

Omnipresent: The Creator is everywhere at all times —he is not someone located in some remote, unknown place. He stands by your side.

Immutable: The Creator never changes—he is the same yesterday, today, and forever.

Truthful: The Creator is absolutely true—it is impossible for him to lie.

Now that you understand the essence of the Creator, you will find it much easier to understand why you can apply the natural laws of the universe in your life and by doing so, accomplish your fondest dreams and never doubt their fulfillment. The Creator established the rules and simply playing the game with all your heart will produce fantastic rewards, that is, if you can *believe!*

Before going on to the next chapter, take these two steps, if you have not already done so:

1. *Convince yourself that there is a happier and more successful way of living than your present way of life.*

2. *Accept the fact that God is a tremendous guiding*

force in this universe and that he is wiser and more powerful than you.

You need not, at this point, accept anything more. But future chapters, hopefully, will help you to accept more and more of the principles that will cause your life to become exceedingly happy and prosperous.

Key Points to Commit to Memory

- Anything you can think of and believe in, you can achieve!
- You may avoid the laws of man, but there are greater laws that cannot be broken.
- Men who have goals and plans dictate to others, while men who have no goals and plans are dictated to.
- Techniques and methods change, but principles never do!
- Quit thinking about all the reasons why you "can't" do something and think of all the reasons why you "can."
- The Creator is sovereign, righteous, just, loving, eternal, omniscient, omnipotent, omnipresent, immutable, and true.

2

Every Man's Dream

If you were asked to define *success*, what would be your answer? Chances are, you have never given it a great deal of thought.

There are probably as many different definitions for success as there are people in the world. Let us consider some of them: If you were to ask a businessman his definition of success, he might say that being successful means earning a lot of money.

A college football coach may believe that the pinnacle of success is winning the National Championship.

To be successful, the pro athlete possibly desires to make the All-Pro team.

To a salesman, success means becoming the number one producer with his company.

Success to the housewife could be her role in her community's ladies' hospital auxiliary.

To the architect, success would probably be beautiful creations on his city's skyline.

A student's dream of success might be that golden moment when he receives his college degree.

The factory worker may feel successful when he

knows he has given his employer a good eight hours of work each day.

To an aspiring young lawyer, a desire to be president may be the ultimate success.

A dentist's dream of success could be a chain of clinics in the city.

To the accountant, success could possibly mean his own office building.

To the minister, success might mean helping someone who is in need.

Success means many things to many people. Everyone may have a personal definition for success, but few have really thought the subject through. Success is more than any of the preceding definitions. It must be considered in greater depth and with a broader spectrum, to reveal the definition of true success.

Success is not merely "money grabbing." This is a shortsighted view because having money does not make a person successful. Al Capone was a millionaire and unsuccessful. One who retires at age forty by chiseling and cheating his or her way to the top is not a successful person. You cannot achieve true success by deluding others.

If you earned a million dollars, but lost your family and home and developed an ulcer in the process—you wouldn't be much of a success.

You would not be successful if you made a million dollars, but died of a heart attack at age forty-three simply because you burned the candle at both ends.

Neither is success living your life on "skid row" in the midst of poverty and disease, as some "anti-establishment" cults might suggest. Nature's laws are a greater force than the mere whims and wishes of man. Truth will always be truth and it cannot be changed.

In this generation we have the so-called "hippies"

who are famous for their "do nothing" attitude. Living under the jurisdiction of natural law as we do, there is no way that these people can find happiness. Neither can they logically be referred to as successful just because they are doing their own thing.

True success avoids extremes! It is a journey. It is a gradual process. It abides in a realm in which balanced living is achieved. Through balanced living you will find happiness and success. Our Creator intends for you and me to lead happy and successful lives by applying the natural laws established by him to keep us in tune with the universe.

If I were to choose one word to define our Creator, the word would be *balance*. Think of the movement of the billions of heavenly bodies throughout the endlessness of space. Each is under perfect control just as precise as the movement of a fine Swiss watch. Consider the perfect balance between the plant and animal worlds, each complementing the other so that both will survive. Yes, our Creator has provided for everything. He is aware of all of our opportunities, as well as all of our problems. He is omniscient!

Thomas Edison understood the essence of our Creator when he made the very profound statement, "Ideas come from space." He planned his life so that he would achieve balance and live within the boundaries of the great natural laws of the universe which cannot be broken without causing adverse effects.

As a schoolboy, Edison was sent home with a note from his teacher saying that he could not learn—that he could not think—that he was stupid. That boy became the world's leading inventor. Edison completely accepted the fact that there was a power in existence bigger than himself and he learned to work in complete harmony with that power.

Great people lead balanced lives which are made meaningful by belief. William B. Walton, president of Holiday Inns, speaking to the Tennessee State Convention of Optimists International, put it this way:

You have four great loves in your life:

1. Love of God—This love puts substance and meaning into your life. This great love enables a man to live with himself. This is the greatest among the four great loves. You must make a total commitment to this love.

2. Love of Family—The love of spouse, children, and relatives is encompassed by this love. This love must be a great love to avoid the problems faced by families in our modern society. It takes a total commitment to gain fulfillment from this great love.

3. Love of Country—You don't inherit a wonderful country like ours. It is passed on from generation to generation, but each new generation must earn the right to keep it. You must develop a fervent love for your country, if you are to be happy and enjoy the fruits of its plentiful bounty. Your love for your country must be a great love, a total commitment.

4. Love of Work—This must be one of your great loves for it provides the sustenance from which you live. To obtain this love you must engage in work that you enjoy and that is fulfilling. By making a total commitment to this great love you can guarantee yourself your share of prosperity.

Surely you can see the threads of direction, balance, and belief woven throughout "The Four Great Loves of

Your Life" as presented by Mr. Walton. During his speech he constantly stressed the importance of attitude as being "the golden key that must be placed in the lock of life." The "Four Great Loves" are simply attitudes about life. His speech certainly exemplifies the thoughts of a man who knows the true definition of success.

Coach Vince Lombardi constantly guided his players with the following statement: "There are only three things that are important in your life!

> Your God,
> your family,
> and the Green Bay Packers."

Again, you should see the threads of direction, balance, and belief woven throughout his statement. Any definition of success must contain these threads of truth or be incomplete.

Success consists of three things if you are to gain a true understanding:

1. Direction—Setting your sights on the things that are worthwhile in life and then establishing a plan to continuously work toward their fulfillment and accomplishment.

2. Balance—Keeping the proper perspective about every area of your life. Staying in harmony with nature's law which produces perfect balance. Balance in all things brings about happiness.

3. Belief—No man will become successful who does not possess belief. The greater his belief—the greater his degree of success. Successful men are believers!

With these three ingredients as a foundation, we will now establish our own definition of success. This will enable us to communicate with complete understanding as we continue through this book. When we refer to success, this is what we mean. Commit these few words to memory. You will carry them with you as a guiding light as long as you live.

"Success is the progressive realization of predetermined, worthwhile goals, stabilized with balance and purified by belief."

Very few people really understand success. Now that *you* do—put it to work in your life!

Here are seven dynamic rules for personal achievement to help you put it to work immediately:

Bland's Dynamic Success Plan

1. *Let God Guide You*—Get yourself out of the way and let the great, universal creative mind of God give you direction—have faith!
2. *Establish a Faith Period*—Set aside thirty golden minutes each morning to engage in meditation and planning.
3. *Crystallize Your Goals*—Decide on specific goals that you want to achieve and keep them before you each day.
4. *Make a Plan of Action*—Develop a blueprint for achieving your goals and a target date for their accomplishment.
5. *Develop a Burning Desire*—Desire for the things you want in life will motivate you to action.
6. *Believe in Yourself*—You can accomplish anything, if you believe you can. You have God-given talents and abilities—use them!
7. *Never Give Up*—Success cannot elude a will that stays in existence in spite of the pressures of adversity. Success comes to persistent people!

It may require changing your entire way of life to

apply the Dynamic Success Plan, but remember, successful men do the things that failures never get around to doing.

Stop! Reread the following parts of this chapter three times. Do this slowly and thoughtfully.

1. The definition of true success.

2. Bland's Dynamic Success Plan.

An hour spent here will be worth many hours later. Accepting these principles takes you another step closer to a life of happiness and prosperity.

Key Points to Commit to Memory

- You cannot achieve true success by deluding others.
- Nature's laws are a greater force than the mere whims and wishes of man.
- Truth will always be truth and it cannot be changed.
- True success avoids extremes!
- Our Creator has provided for everything.
- Great people lead balanced lives which are made meaningful by belief.
- Success is the progressive realization of predetermined, worthwhile goals, stabilized with balance and purified by belief!

3

Building Your Success Complex

Whether you weigh 150 pounds or 300 pounds, you possess in common with every other adult about forty-eight ounces of absolutely fantastic tissue. Carefully protected by the cranium, this is the most intricate and baffling computer ever conceived. This is your mind! You own this unique computer lock, stock, and barrel. It can produce happiness and success for you in unbelievable proportions.

This tremendous data processing center, which you carry with you wherever you go, is the last great unexplored "continent" on the earth. The riches that will arise from its exploration will be beyond comparison.

This fantastic computer of yours was designed and created by God's infinite intelligence. It is capable of processing data stored in the world's memory bank which contains all information—from the past, the present, and on into eternity. Your mind can conceive of any idea you will ever need.

If one were to invent a mechanical computer with the endless potential of the human mind, the cost of using it would be so prohibitive that it would be impractical to put it into production. This may give you an idea of the value of the human mind, which despite its wealth-giving potential, is used by most people at about 10 percent of its potential. We occupy our minds with insignificant things instead of letting them soar, as they were divinely designed to do, to accomplish big and important things.

Industry employs people known as computer programmers to plan and screen information fed into computers. The computer can return information based only on the information it is given by the programmer. If the programmer does his work well, the information received will be worthwhile and useful; if he fails to write the program correctly, the information produced will be negative and useless. The human mind is no different! Your mind is the computer and you are the computer programmer. If you put positive information in, the results will be positive and worthwhile. If you feed your mind-computer negative information, the results will be negative and directed toward failure.

You are the sum total of your own thoughts. If you think in negative terms, you will achieve negative results, but if you think in positive terms, you will achieve positive results.

Wise men and philosophers throughout the ages have disagreed about many things, but they are unanimously in agreement on one point: *"We become what we think about!"*

Emerson said, "A man is what he thinks about all day long."

The Roman emperor Marcus Aurelius put it this way, "A man's life is what his thoughts make of it."

William James said, "The greatest discovery of my generation is that human beings can alter their lives by altering their attitudes of mind."

In the Bible, we find: "As a man thinks in his heart, so is he."

You *are* guided by your mind and you must live upon the fruits of your thoughts in the future. Since "we become what we think about," then it is most important that we carefully regard our thought patterns. This is one of the most powerful natural laws in the universe. You will find this law to be a two-edged sword—a natural law that can lead a man to a life of inner peace, wealth, enlightenment, and physical well-being, and a law that can lead him into the gutter into a life of misery.

How the law works for you depends on how you use it—for good or for evil—the choice is yours. Never forget that you live in a world of cause and effect—for every action, there is a reaction. Or as the Bible states it, "As you sow, so shall you reap!"

People and things will respond and behave for us according to the pattern of our own thoughts.

Most of us try to change other people. To achieve our goals, we do not need to change others, we need to change ourselves. Others change as we change our thoughts about them.

Developing right thinking is not easy because it involves establishing new habits which take days, weeks, months, and often years before they become an integral part of our life. New habits are not easily formed, especially when they must replace entrenched bad habits. The task is not easy, but it *can* be done. If you strive to be happy and successful, you must establish good habits, because while in the beginning you make your habits, in the end your habits make you. Each of us has bad habits and negative thoughts that hold us back and keep us from becoming the dynamic person that lives within.

How do these bad habits and negative thoughts begin? In many cases, they stem from childhood. For example, I remember members of my family saying, "There never has been a rich Bland and there never will be." This I believed for many years because my mind had been programmed to accept the fact that I, being a Bland, could not become wealthy. Being in an environment with negative people can overcome you with their negativism. In society, this occurs when we conform to the life of the followers rather than becoming a leader. Much of the trash found on bookstore shelves will program you for failure. Much of the entertainment available today can have a negative impact upon your thinking.

I could list countless reasons why a person lives in a negative world, but I am more interested in communicating to you the process which will enable you to put away the cloak of failure worn in the negative life, and to replace it with a beautiful shiny new suit of armor called *success doctrine*.

How can you get your suit of armor? The first step to acquiring success doctrine is your making a decision that you want to become happy, successful, and to possess great wisdom. If you, like most of us, have been programmed for failure from childhood, you will need to re-program your thinking so that you can truly hold the key to happiness in your hand—the wisdom of the ages! You will not gain this wisdom overnight—your negative thoughts will not suddenly disappear. It will take time to replace negativism with positiveness. It is a gradual process and may take from one to three years depending upon your ability.

When you begin this wonderful new way of living, there will be times you will mentally lapse into your former negative world, but you will have the strength to get back on the track once you realize what has happened. As your wisdom and knowledge increase, negative mental lapses will decrease until they disappear entirely from your happy and successful life.

Now that we have established that thoughts have power, that thoughts become reality, and that by programming your mind with positive thoughts, you can become a positive person, let me explain how to build a success complex in your life.

The Success Complex

Step 6 Mastery of the Details of Life
Step 5 Capacity to Love
Step 4 Relaxed Mental Attitude
Step 3 Inner Happiness
Step 2 Success Oriented
Step 1 Success Doctrine (Wisdom)

Step 1: Let us imagine for a moment that you are a master builder and you have been commissioned to construct a six-story building. You select the strongest supports and the best materials in designing the foundation. Without a firm foundation, the structure cannot stand; it would crumble and fall. The full weight of the other five stories will rest upon this firm foundation.

Upon the firm foundation of success doctrine (wisdom) all of the worthwhile things in life rest. Success doctrine will stabilize and sustain you through your greatest accomplishments and your bitterest adversities. Each of us will have good fortune smile on us in many ways before we die, but we must also realize that we will face several major setbacks during our lifetime.

Without a success doctrine in your life, you could easily find yourself off the right track and headed for failure.

Success doctrine is a strong foundation on which your future should be built. The Bible says, "Wisdom gives: A long, good life—riches—honor—pleasure—peace" (Proverbs 3:16-17). "He who loves wisdom loves his own best interest and will be a success" (Proverbs 19:8).

You gain wisdom by becoming a student. You read, you study, you listen and you must do these things each day on a planned and organized basis. You will be provided a list of books for required reading and study. These books have been especially selected to provide you with a source of success doctrine. It must become a part of your life—you must eat, sleep and drink success doctrine—it is good for the soul. "I, Wisdom, will make the hours of your day more profitable and the years of your life more fruitful" (Proverbs 9:11). *Believe* and these promises are yours for the taking!

Step 2: You will be success oriented when you have success doctrine foremost in your mind. You will understand yourself and because you do, you can then begin to understand others. Others will come to you because you possess a complete understanding of the natural laws of the universe and you have the right answers. You will find you "have a way" with people and that you can make exciting things happen in business. Your family life will improve, your business life will improve, your spiritual life will improve. The world will truly be your "oyster" for you will have become a wise person—one who possesses the wisdom of the ages—a man who *believes!*

Step 3: Everyone in the world seems to be searching

for inner happiness. You can find inner happiness as soon as you possess success doctrine and become success oriented. Because you completely understand the Creator and his natural laws, your life will be in complete harmony with the world around you. This generates an inner peace and happiness that will radiate forth like the glow of a candle in a window on a dark night. Inner happiness will be yours along with the other blessings which accompany it—*believe!*

Step 4: Once you have success doctrine in the frontal lobe of your mind and have become success oriented and possess inner happiness, you will develop a relaxed mental attitude. You will be able to cope with every situation without frustration or anxiety. Virtually nothing will "shake you up" because you will possess a relaxed mental attitude. You will then have everything under control.

If you are a salesman, you will not become discouraged when your most important appointment is broken. If you are a businessman or woman, you will not let the rigors of each day pull you apart. If you are a wife and mother, you will not "blow your stack" because of home pressures placed on you. If you are an athlete, you will "keep your cool" during the heat of fierce competition while others become frantic. Yes, you will be able to master every situation, for you will be the possessor of a relaxed mind.

The Bible says: "A relaxed attitude lengthens a man's life" (Proverbs 14:30). Belief fosters a relaxed mind!

Step 5: The next important step in the success complex is acquiring the capacity to love. Do not confuse this with the selfish, humanistic love found so often in society today. If everyone had the capacity to love others, based upon the sure foundation of success doctrine, there would be no racial prejudice, no wars, no need for policemen, and everyone would respect everyone else for what he and she is.

This is the true, complete and unselfish love, the kind the Apostle Paul talked about in the 13th and 14th chapters of First Corinthians: "If I had the gift of being able to speak in other languages without learning them, and could speak in every language there is in all of heaven and earth, but didn't love others, I would only be making noise. If I had the gift of prophecy and knew all about what is going to happen in the future, knew everything about everything, but didn't love others, what good would it do? Even if I had the gift of faith so that I could speak to a mountain and make it move, I would still be worth nothing at all without love. If I gave everything I have to poor people, and if I were burned alive for preaching the Gospel but didn't love others, it would be of no value whatever.

"Love is very patient and kind, never jealous or envious, never boastful or proud, never haughty or selfish or rude. Love does not demand its own way. It is not irritable or touchy. It does not hold grudges and will hardly even notice when others do it wrong. It is never glad about injustice, but rejoices whenever truth wins out. If you love someone you will be loyal to him no matter what the cost. You will always believe in him, always expect the best of him, and always stand your ground in defending him.

"All the special gifts and powers from God will someday come to an end, but love goes on forever.

"There are three things that remain—faith, hope, and love—and the greatest of these is love."

Even as great a man as the Apostle Paul readily admitted that without the capacity to love, everything else is meaningless. With success doctrine, you will have a much deeper and more meaningful feeling for your family and your fellow men—*believe!*

Step 6: The pinnacle of the success complex is occupied by the mastery of the details of life, a gift to all who possess the success complex. Most people find it difficult to meet the daily trials and tribulations, but those who possess success doctrine know how to organize themselves through goals, plans and priorities to handle anything that comes up. The little things drive most people up the wall, but the individual with success doctrine accepts each little thing as a challenge. He learns to solve what he can and to live with what he can't without destroying his peace of mind. The man who believes is master over all.

Now that you have the structure of the success complex, I hope that you will begin to put it to work in your life. You will find the results fantastic.

Most people want to be success oriented, have inner happiness, display a relaxed mental attitude, possess the capacity to love, and want to be able to master the details of life. Few are willing to pay the price of gaining the success doctrine. They want to eat the frosting, but they don't want to take the time and trouble to bake the cake. The good things in life cannot be yours unless you pay the price to obtain them. That price is success doctrine. Please *believe* you don't get something for nothing.

Before going on to the next chapter, you must accept the following principles:

1. *You are the product of your own thoughts!*
2. *You are capable of conceiving every idea you will ever need.*
3. *You can change others simply by changing yourself.*
4. *You can become success oriented—have inner*

happiness—display a relaxed mental attitude—
possess the capacity to love—and master the
details of life—by acquiring success doctrine
(wisdom).

Accepting these principles takes you another step closer
to a life of happiness and prosperity.

Key Points to Commit to Memory

- We become what we think about!
- People and things will respond and behave for us according to the pattern of our own thoughts.
- In the beginning you make your habits, but in the end your habits make you.
- Success doctrine will stabilize and sustain you through your greatest accomplishments and your bitterest adversities.
- The good things in life cannot be yours unless you pay the price to obtain them.
- Please *believe* you don't get something for nothing.

4

You Need
a Blueprint
for Success

Imagine that you are an internationally known architect and that you have just received a contract to supervise the construction of the world's tallest and most beautiful building.

Your first task would be to estimate the quantity and quality of the materials required for this fabulous structure.

Then, your next step would be to ask the contractors to hire the skilled craftsmen—the steel workers, the carpenters, the brick layers, and plumbers and electricians and the common laborers required to complete the gigantic undertaking.

Now let's suppose that you are at the building site. The building materials are piled high, the contractors are surrounded by their workmen. You give the command, "Build me a building!" The first question on the lips of every craftsman and the contractors for whom they work would be, "Where is the blueprint?"

If each of these men began work on this great building using his own individual thought, the building would live in history as a monstrosity.

There would be no organized effort toward one

common objective because the craftsmen would be "going off in all directions at the same time." The most likely thing to happen would be that the building would never be completed. Confusion and frustration would reign.

When each craftsman endeavored to do his own thing, it would be impossible to work together and—with no blueprint—the entire idea would be lost.

The project, which in the planning could be one of the great wonders of the world, would never get off the ground.

A master craftsman *must* have a plan! He cannot effectively use his talents unless he has guidelines to direct his genius. He must have a blueprint if he is going to construct a thing of beauty.

Your own life is a direct parallel to the building that we have been describing. You are the architect. You can construct happiness and success or a life filled with misery and failure. The blueprint is the key to the results. You must have a plan if you are going to succeed! Without a blueprint to guide your efforts, you end up confused, disillusioned and totally frustrated.

People with goals and plans succeed in life, while people without them fail. A leading New York medical doctor recently declared, "After examining 15,321 men and women in New York City, I came to see that the major problem of these patients was lack of values and objectives in life."

There are thousands of men in the medical profession throughout the world who could make the same statement. We are living at a point in world history when people restlessly wander about looking for something that can't be explained. They are confused. They are frustrated. They are filled with anxiety, and can't understand why.

There is only one solution. We must go back to the fundamentals. Any outstanding athlete will tell you that he must periodically go back to fundamentals if he is to remain on top—if he doesn't, his play becomes sloppy, his skills become ineffective. Every champion boxer who retained his championship went back to road work and sparring partners before every fight. When overconfidence prevailed and basics were eliminated, defeat followed.

Like the athlete, man must go back to basic fundamentals of skillful living given to him by the Creator— the great natural laws of the universe. In Ecclesiastes 7:13 you find the following gem of wisdom: "See the way the Creator does things and fall into line. Don't fight the facts of nature." You can't beat him; many who were more capable than you and I have tried and failed, so you may as well join him and let his natural laws work for you and not against you!

One of the best known natural laws of the universe is the law of gravity. You know that if you climb to the top of a tall building and jump off, you will fall downward—you never fall upward! You can't see the law of gravity, you can't smell the law of gravity, nor can you touch the law of gravity—but you know it is there. So it is with the great natural laws of happiness and success— you can't see them, smell them, or touch them, but they are there.

You can operate within the framework of these laws, and happiness and success will be yours for the taking. The Creator has certain objectives that will be accomplished through mankind and he has a plan to guarantee their fulfillment. The Holy Bible is the Creator's plan for the ages. Everything has been laid out in great detail beginning with Genesis and ending with Revelation—it is all there—just as the Creator planned it.

Notice that even the greatest power in the universe, the Creator, has established goals and has made plans to attain them. Since we are his creation and all are fully under the jurisdiction of his natural laws, we should follow his example by setting definite goals and designing specific personal plans for their fulfillment. It works for the Creator—it will work for you!

Goals and plans are the magic keys to happiness and success! Only 3 percent of all people have goals and plans and write them down. Ten percent more have goals and plans, but keep them in their heads. The rest—87 percent—drift through life without definite goals or plans. They do not know where they are going and others dictate to them.

Let's examine these statistics further. The 3 percent who have goals and plans that are written down accomplish from fifty to one hundred times more during their life than the 10 percent who have goals and plans and merely keep them in their heads. These statistics alone should motivate you to set definite personal goals, establish a plan of action for their fulfillment, and then commit both your goals and plans to writing. Please note, the Creator committed his goals and plans to writing in the Holy Bible!

You *must* have goals and plans. Prisons are full of unfortunate people who had no goals and plans and one day each found himself outside the boundaries of man's laws. This would never occur to individuals with goals and plans established within the perimeter of those laws greater than man's—natural law. Goals and plans made within the framework of natural law take the worry out of living. Conformity to God's laws frees your mind so that you may get on with your opportunities.

There are four reasons most people don't set goals and establish plans:

1. They don't know how.
2. It's too much trouble.
3. They don't have faith in their goals and plans after they are developed.
4. They begin on a long-range basis and this prevents them from seeing immediate results, so they become discouraged.

If one of these reasons is holding you back, the Bland Method of Goal Setting and Planning will solve your problem. My method is the simplest and most efficient ever devised. It teaches you the principles of short-range and long-range planning, enabling you to discover immediately that planning really works.

My method is not founded on the laws of man. It is based on natural law, which will give you the confidence and faith you need to stick with the program. My method is the way to a happy and successful life. All you need to do is to put it to work for you.

You must really want to set goals and to plan for their attainment. No one can force you to do it. After you decide that goal setting and planning are for you, take time to establish definite goals and plans for yourself. You will find that the most difficult part of the process is carrying out your plans once they have been committed to writing.

In the beginning, you will find yourself getting off the track many times, but if you stick with the program, you will remain on your basic course. Depending upon your own ability, it will take from one to three years before your mind will be sufficiently programmed to carry out every minute detail of your plans.

You will encounter temporary defeat many times,

but by sticking with the program you will charge through adverse situations like an All-Pro running back on his way to the goal line. Remember this principle, "Out of every adversity comes an equal or greater opportunity"—it never fails.

This principle was clearly illustrated in Houston, Texas, several years ago. A great sports arena was planned, the first of its kind. A glass roof would cover the arena so that sporting events could be conducted under perfect climatic conditions despite Mother Nature.

When the magnificent structure was completed, Mother Nature retaliated. Grass would not grow on the playing field. The developers had a multimillion-dollar sports complex, built to house professional football and baseball, that had become worthless simply because grass would not grow.

Applying the principle, the builders attacked the problem. This adversity resulted in the discovery of an artificial playing surface which experts say is even better than grass. Today, artificial turf covers many out-of-door stadiums across our nation.

"Out of every adversity comes an equal or greater opportunity," is simply another way of saying that necessity is the mother of invention. You will find that what appears a permanent obstacle in the way of your desires is only a figment of your imagination. The Bible says, "You are a poor specimen if you can't stand the pressure of adversity" (Proverbs 24:10). Welcome adversity; it is your springboard to great achievement!

As you begin to formulate goals in your mind, dare to think big! A wise man once said, "It is better to aim your arrow at a star and hit an eagle, than to aim your arrow at an eagle and hit a stone." For example, let's say that my income for the past year was $15,000 and I was not pleased with the figure. I set a goal for the coming year of $35,000 which was much better to fit my needs. After working hard to attain my new income objective, I found that I had earned only $28,483. Did I fail? Certainly not! True, I did not attain my $35,000 income goal, but look at the fantastic progress that was made.

Dare to aim high—shoot for the moon as long as you sincerely believe you can reach your goal at some time in the future. Don't concern yourself too much with how you are going to achieve your goal. Leave that completely to a Power greater than yourself.

Emerson said, "Assume in your imagination it is already yours, the goal you aspire to have; enter into the part enthusiastically, live the character just as does the great actor absorb the character he plays."

It is wise to use the counsel of other qualified people when you set your goals and make your plans. In Proverbs 15:22 we find the following wisdom, "Plans go wrong with too few counselors; many counselors bring success."

I would suggest that you choose one or two individuals whose judgment and ability you greatly respect and form a Success Council for the purpose of exchanging ideas regarding each individual's personal goals and plans.

The Bible also says, "The intelligent man is always open to new ideas. In fact, he looks for them" (Proverbs 18:15). So when you form your alliance, choose one or two others who can help you grow through the association. When two minds get together, their interaction seems to create a third "mind" which produces very creative thoughts and solves many problems.

"Two can accomplish more than twice as much as one, for the results can be much better. If one falls, the other pulls him up; but if a man falls when he is alone,

47

he's in trouble. And one standing alone can be attacked and defeated, but two can stand back-to-back and conquer; three is even better, for a triple braided cord is not easily broken" (Ecclesiastes 4:9, 12). "Be with wise men and become wise" (Proverbs 13:20).

A Success Council to assist you in goal setting can be of great value.

1. To function properly, there must be complete harmony among its members.
2. There can be no negativism, or the group will become a negative force which will destroy each individual involved. To succeed, the Success Council must function in a proper positive atmosphere. Stay away from negative people because they will program you for failure.
3. Guide group thinking by establishing positive guidelines.
4. Schedule regular meetings with time for each member to make a personal progress report. This provides the follow-through necessary for individual goals and plans to become reality.

Just setting a goal and making your plans to attain it are not enough. You must also decide when you wish to attain the goal. Set a date—it could be as short as an hour, a day, a week, or a month. It could be one year, five years, or at age sixty-five. Who knows? But you must establish this target date if your goal is to become a reality.

In 1960 President John F. Kennedy addressed the nation, announcing the beginning of a ten-year space program designed to put a man on the moon.

Let's analyze why this effort was such a huge success. First, a definite goal was selected—a man on the moon!

Second, there was a basic plan to follow. Many

problems were without answers, but there was a starting place—a basic plan.

Third, there was a target date—ten years in which to make this dream a reality.

There was a fourth procedure employed on this project. Although we have not yet discussed it, it is a fundamental part of goal setting. After the first three steps—a goal, a plan and a target date—it was necessary to constantly keep the goal before them each day. This made it positive that the goal would become a reality. This principle is discussed at greater length in the Plan of Action section.

Men and women engaged in the moonshot project worked together toward the fulfillment of their goal day by day. They did not know exactly how they would put a man on the moon, but they had faith and believed that it could be done. They did not know exactly what the space ship would look like and they never conceived how great a part computers would play in the positive outcome of the project.

There were many unknowns, but they kept their goal constantly before them. They used group thinking, and maintained their faith through temporary defeat. Because they believed that their goal would be accomplished, the answers came and the United States successfully landed a man on the moon with one year to spare.

The tremendous achievement in reaching the moon should convince you that never again should you doubt the wisdom of goal setting and planning. The space program applied every principle for successful goal setting and so there was no way for the project to fail— a man was put on the moon!

Let me repeat the steps the space project took:

1. A goal was set.
2. A plan was made.
3. A firm target date was established.
4. Group thinking was employed.
5. Everyone kept the goal constantly in mind.
6. Action was applied.
7. They fervently kept the faith.

The result: It was impossible for them to fail!

Before going on to the next chapter, you must accept the following principles:

1. *Think **big!***
2. *Plan to avoid chaos.*
3. *Seek opportunity in adversity.*
4. *Join the 3 percent with **written** plans and multiply your results.*
5. *Create a Success Council to make sure your written plan works.*

Accepting these principles takes you another step closer to a life of happiness and prosperity.

Key Points to Commit to Memory

- People with goals and plans succeed in life, while people without them fail.
- Goals and plans are the magic keys to happiness and success.
- Goals and plans made within the framework of natural law take the worry out of living.
- Out of every adversity comes an equal or greater opportunity.
- You will find that what appears a permanent obstacle in the way of your desires is only a figment of your imagination.
- Dare to think big!

5

Life's Tightrope: Spiritual and Financial Balance

Areas One and Two

Now we reach the most important phase of the goal setting and planning process—the part that affects true happiness. The principles already presented will bring into your life an abundance of material wealth. But those principles will *not* bring happiness. True happiness can only be achieved by living a balanced life.

Have you ever watched a performer on a tightrope? He steps out firmly, but carefully, his balancing pole is tilted from side to side, ever so slightly, as he inches his way along. His eye never leaves the tightrope. It guides him to safety, just as surely as do his perfectly balanced muscles and movements. Diverting his eyes or exaggerating any movement can mean disaster, perhaps his life.

Balance is the key for the performer and for us. All of the natural laws brought into being by the Creator are based on the natural law of balance. As I stated previously, "If I had to select one word to describe the Creator, that word would be *balance.*" Since the law of balance applies to all of nature—the universe, animal life, plant life, and everything that exists—it certainly applies to you and to me. When the law of balance is broken in the natural world—nature suffers! When the law of balance is broken in man's world—man suffers!

Each of us needs to learn to live within the boundaries of this great natural law. Guided by the law of balance in your life, you will create more happiness than you had ever dreamed possible. If you are in balance with the world around you, you will be happy! If you are out of balance with the world around you— you will be unhappy! Isn't that simple? Extremely simple, but extremely important!

Let me show you how to use the law of balance in your life so that you may enjoy the abundant happiness that it will shower down upon you. Your life is made up of four major areas:

> Spiritual
> Financial
> Educational
> Recreational

If you want happiness to radiate around you, you must learn to set goals and make plans in each of these four areas. Without proper blend and emphasis upon these four areas, your life will be out of balance—you will be unhappy.

Let's explore each of these four areas which so vitally control your life.

Area One: Spiritual Balance

Do you know someone who is spiritually out of balance? Perhaps you know someone so obsessed with things of a spiritual nature that he is a fanatic. As a result, people do not want to associate with him. They avoid him and he cannot accomplish his total purpose for one reason—he is overbalanced in one area. Perhaps you know someone who, in great contrast, has *no* spiritual life. He leads a very loose existence and he is unhappy because he has no real friends. His activities are not conducive to founding genuine friendship. These examples are two extremes, but each illustrates clearly the problem of spiritual imbalance.

Any twentieth-century thinking man can arrive at an intelligent conclusion that there is a Supreme Being—a powerful God, an intelligent God with complete authority over all things.

The prophet Isaiah, in his inspired book in the Bible, records the following words from the Creator: "For there is no other God but me—a just God and a Savior—no, not one! Let all the world look to me for salvation! For I am God; there is no other" (Isaiah 45:21-22).

Man's very nature embodies an innate drive to worship something. This worship takes many different forms—both idealistic and materialistic—but the Bible says there should be only one object of worship and the true object is the Creator. When man's eyes are on the Creator, his life will flow with milk and honey! Why fight it? Get on the team and play the game with all your heart and you will find happiness and success. Make definite spiritual plans for you and your family to enjoy the balanced fullness and meaningfulness of life. You will never be sorry—*believe!*

Area Two: Financial Balance

Perhaps you have a friend who is financially out of balance. This individual is driven by money alone. Money is an obsession and the pursuit of it has caused a complete collapse of his personal life and family harmony. Men lose their friends, end up becoming broken, miserable individuals because of money.

In 1923, nine of the world's most successful financiers met at Chicago's Edgewater Beach Hotel. Financially, they literally "held the world by the tail"—anything that money could buy was within their grasp—they were rich—rich—rich! Read their names and the high position each held:

1. Charles Schwab, the president of the largest steel company.
2. Samuel Insull, the president of the largest electric utility company.
3. Howard Hopson, the president of the largest gas company.
4. Arthur Cutten, the greatest wheat speculator.
5. Richard Whitney, the president of the New York Stock Exchange.
6. Albert Fall, the Secretary of Interior in President Harding's Cabinet.
7. Jesse Livermore, the greatest "bear" on Wall Street.
8. Ivar Kreuger, head of the world's greatest monopoly.
9. Leon Fraser, president of the Bank of International Settlements.

A tremendously impressive group—right? Would you like to change positions with one of them? Before you decide, let's look at the picture 25 years later—in 1948:

1. Charles Schwab was forced into bankruptcy and lived the last five years before his death on borrowed money.
2. Samuel Insull not only died in a foreign land, a fugitive from justice, but was penniless.
3. Howard Hopson was insane.

4. Arthur Cutten became insolvent and had died abroad.
5. Richard Whitney had just been released from Sing Sing prison.
6. Albert Fall had been pardoned from prison so he could die at home—broke.
7. Jesse Livermore had died a suicide.
8. Ivar Kreuger took his own life.
9. Leon Fraser also committed suicide.

Now, are you still impressed with this group? A vast amount of talent and potential went down the drain with these men. What happened?

Their lives were out of balance!

Wise King Solomon wrote: "The rich man thinks of his wealth as an impregnable defense, a high wall of safety. What a dreamer!" (Proverbs 18:11). King Solomon was well-known, not only for his wisdom but his great wealth.

In Ecclesiastes 5:10, we find: "He who loves money shall never have enough. The foolishness of thinking that wealth brings happiness!"

In the opposite extreme, you find an individual to whom money means nothing. He fails to provide for his own and he lives in poverty. He depends on charity to provide the necessities of life. This individual has just as serious a financial imbalance as the individual who is "money mad." Somewhere in between these two extremes there is a place of perfect balance— where you can have money and be happy!

In almost every case, the single biggest problem these people faced was the handling of money. Most people simply don't understand that they cannot have both money and things—at least, in the beginning! To accumulate money, you must give up things. But if you accumulate things, you will never have money. It is just that simple and yet few people really understand it.

King Solomon put it this way: "A man who loves pleasure becomes poor; wine and luxury are not the way of riches!" (Proverbs 21:17). This came from a man who probably accumulated more riches than anyone in all history.

If you sincerely want to accumulate money, there are seven things you must do:

1. *Don't charge*—Take your credit cards, put a rubber band around them, place them in the bottom of your chest of drawers and forget them. Charge accounts and credit cards get people into financial trouble and there are countless cases to prove the point. Remember: "Just as the rich rule the poor, so the borrower is servant to the lender" (Proverbs 22:7).

2. *Don't consolidate your bills*—In theory, this is a popular thing to do, but it does not always work out the way you plan. You may consolidate bills into one monthly payment at extremely high interest rates and then end up with the new consolidated debt to pay, plus many new ones. The new debts have been created because the old, bad money management habits have not been changed.

If you are deeply in debt, work out a repayment plan and call all of your creditors and inform them of your plan and assure them that they will be paid. You will find them very willing to work with you.

3. *Don't buy impulsively*—Place a small blackboard on your kitchen wall. When you desire to purchase anything of consequence, write it down on the blackboard. Wait one month and then, if you still want it, consider working it into your budget. In most instances you will discover that your desire was only a passing fancy.

4. *Establish a budget*—Purchase a ledger and begin to keep records of your income and expenses. Decide exactly what you will spend for necessities and luxuries each month and then stick with it. Watch every penny! There exists a proven principle which says, "If you can't live on $500 per month—you couldn't live on $5,000 per month." You say, "Maybe so, but I sure would like to try!" The truth is that the principle is the same—if you have financial problems living on $500 per month, you will have the same problems trying to live on $5,000 a month. You see, your same old bad money management habits will cause you to over-spend when earning $5,000, just as they did when you were earning $500. The only difference is that you will create much bigger problems when earning $5,000. Think about this principle—it's true!

5. *Pay yourself first*—Every time you receive your paycheck, put something aside for yourself. At first, the amount may be small, perhaps only a dollar a week, but this will grow because you are forming a good habit—the habit of saving. William B. Johnson began to save his pennies during the early 1900's. These pennies grew into dollars and then into hundreds of dollars. When the great depression came, he used his savings to take advantage of the misfortune of others. He purchased their land at distressed prices. He became a wealthy land baron only because he developed the habit of saving his money, which enabled him to take advantage of opportunity.

In Proverbs 21:20, we find this appropriate statement: "The wise man saves for the future, but the foolish man spends whatever he gets." Your creditors will wait for their money, they do not have any other choice, so pay yourself first—*save*.

There are many little games that you can play which

will trick yourself into saving. Try this one: Set an empty coffee can in your bedroom and empty into it the change from your pocket each night. When you cash a check, make it for a dollar more and put it into savings. Originate some games such as these and then play them to help you save money. Your goal should be at least 10 percent of your earnings.

6. *How to pay monthly bills*—When you write checks each month, write them in this order:

    a. Church or some worthwhile charity.

    b. Savings.

    c. Insurance for security.

    d. Food.

    e. Shelter.

    f. All other things.

This procedure works like a charm. It will help you focus upon providing for the necessary things first and then letting all of the other things take care of themselves. Have faith, try it!

7. *Investing*—Permit me to outline for you these five steps to good money management. This procedure has never failed to accumulate wealth. Putting these five steps to work will provide financial security in your life:

    a. *Basic needs*—As you begin your journey to accumulated wealth, you must provide food, clothing, and shelter before investing in other things. Some never progress beyond providing these basic needs for their families, but for those who do, the next step is:

    b. *Insurance*—As you plan toward financial success, you must protect yourself from possible financial disasters with life, health, and casualty insurance. They protect you from financial ruin. Some people manage to provide basic needs and insurance but never get beyond that plateau. For those who do, the next step is:

c. *Cash fund*—As you grow financially, you need to build a cash fund for emergencies and opportunities that come along. Open a savings account and build it until it equals six months of your income. Some people provide basic needs, insurance, and the cash fund but never get beyond this level. For those who go beyond this on the money accumulation scale, the next step is:

d. *Unimproved land*—Investing money in unimproved land will provide a relatively safe investment with a very high return. The amount of land available is limited and as the population explosion increases, it will become more and more scarce. The land owner eventually will once again rule society, just as he did before the industrial revolution. The value of land should never decrease, so at this point in your accumulation of wealth—buy unimproved land. Some people provide for the basic needs, insurance, cash fund, and unimproved land, and never proceed farther. For those who do, the next step is:

e. *Stocks and bonds*—The final step in accumulating wealth is the purchase of stocks and bonds. This is properly the last step because it is a speculative investment. This step can prove to be risky and caution should always be exercised when engaging in this type of investment.

These are the five steps to good money management. They will work for you to bring you the riches that they have brought many others. Normally the only problem arises when you decide that the five steps are too slow. You decide that you want to "make it quick" and jump all the way to step five. When you do so, look out! You are headed for financial disaster. Stick with the five steps—they work!

There is an ancient myth concerning money that is very easily destroyed. The Bible does *not* say that money is evil. The Bible does say, "The love of money is the root of all evil" (1 Timothy 6:10, KJV).

Man has the choice. He earns money by rendering service and he has the freedom to use money as he pleases. If he uses money for worthwhile things—then money is good. But if he uses it in a way that deludes himself or others, then money has become evil. Money cannot choose how it will be used. Man is the key. Man has to make the choice.

Ministers sometimes deliver messages, damning money as being evil, and then, at the close of the sermon, appeal to the congregation for more contributions to the church budget. If money is evil, then why is it needed to keep the doors of the church open? It is evident that money is not evil, but man can make it evil.

It takes money to accomplish just about anything worthwhile in life. It takes money to print and publish good literature. It takes money to support churches, hospitals, and educational institutions. It takes money to provide for the underprivileged and poverty stricken. It takes money to pass the Bland Method of Goal Setting and Planning on to you. Money is good and useful when man keeps his motives right and chooses to use money for worthwhile causes.

When you begin to accumulate money in large amounts, you will face a new problem. Many good and evil opportunities, never available to you before, will tempt you. Suddenly, the world will be at your doorstep with every temptation imaginable. If you have sound goals and plans, having a large amount of money and being tempted will not disturb your happiness and peace of mind. Without goals and plans to stabilize you, you will be doomed.

Jesus said, "It is easier for a camel to go through the eye of a needle than for a rich man to enter the kingdom of the Creator." This pointed out that the temptation to do evil is very great when you have an abundance of money and that if you become a slave to money, it will destroy your peace of mind and your relationship with the Creator.

When that relationship has been disturbed, you will be out of balance with the great natural laws of the universe and you will forfeit the good life that is available to you. But this need not happen if you have firmly entrenched sound goals and plans to guide you.

Many rich men who have gone on before and countless others living today have entered into the kingdom of perfect peace and harmony that the Creator planned for them. While it may be difficult for the rich to achieve perfect balance, it can be done through goals and plans which keep the pathway to happiness and success open.

The way in which you regard money is extremely important. When the love of money becomes all-important, you have financial imbalance. Money has become the master rather than the slave. Applying the law of balance in your life will teach you to keep money in proper perspective and safeguard your happiness and success.

No man can attain riches unless he enriches others. Study the success stories of the great men and you will find that many of them were very generous with their wealth. J. C. Penney and R. G. LeTourneau built vast wealth, but each attributed much of his success to sharing his good fortune with others.

I have discussed the principle of sharing with many successful businessmen. They have told me they would be literally afraid not to give—the consequences are too great. Happy and successful men will tell you quickly that "You can't outgive the Giver!" This is a natural law. This is referred to many times by the Bible as well as many other sources. "It is possible to give away and become richer! It is also possible to hold on too tightly and lose everything. Yes, the liberal man shall be rich! By watering others, he waters himself" (Proverbs 11:24-25). I know men who give away 40 or 50 percent of their earnings and I have been told about others who give away four of every five dollars they earn. Naturally, these individuals are wealthy and can afford to give away much of their income, but these men have always made giving a habit—even when they were poor. Giving is one of the natural laws that they used to accumulate their wealth.

The Bible tells us that the Creator loves a cheerful giver and will return his gifts many times over if the gifts are given with the right attitude. You can't give with the expectation of getting. Your gift must be given freely with no strings attached. When gifts are given unselfishly, with nothing expected in return, they will be returned many times over. Gifts, without the proper attitude of giving, are meaningless.

The size of the gift is not important. But the attitude with which it is given is extremely important. If you give in the manner in which the Creator intends for us to give, you will be rewarded generously.

Thinking in terms of wealth and giving to others so soon after discussing the five steps to good money management may seem out of place. This has been done intentionally and the following example of a substantial giver in action will prove the point:

Jess Radle trudged behind his mule as the plow kicked up showers of dust. These forty acres, without water except for scattered sprinkles in recent months, held little promise for his bride of three months. The food in the house just might stretch till Saturday, three days off. The shed had less than a measure of feed for the mule. Jess stopped, mopped the sweat from his brow. Dust caked, reddish brown, in the furrows of his face. Hat in hand, he tilted his head back and looked to the sky. "Lord, if you'll send a dollar my way, I'll always see that you get your share."

Now a wealthy rancher, he recalled this incident for my benefit. He had just gratefully made a substantial contribution to one of his charities. The gift was one of many over the years. At first, they were only coins, then bills and eventually checks that have grown and grown as he prospered. "You know, it didn't start to rain down money on me and my mule. And we didn't have any more to eat at sundown than we had before. But somehow that mule plowed better; that ground held the moisture better, and we made it out of the depression. But I'll tell you one thing—I like to give, I enjoy sharing with others—but mister, I'd be lying if I didn't say I'd be afraid not to give after the promise I made."

Just where are you going to get the money so that you can start giving some away?

There is only one source—the money you earn. That must come from some beneficial service you can render to your fellow man. You will be rewarded in direct proportion to the service you render—no more, no less!

Do you need to find some new service to render? Probably not. Most people can render a beneficial service in their present work. When men want to earn more money, their first impulse is to find a better job, a greener pasture. All too often, a change in occupation results in the discovery that the grass was not really that much greener on the other side of the fence. And, usually, the change has made things worse instead of better.

You probably have a virtual gold mine right where you are. Don't overlook the obvious. Establish your goals and make your plans to render the best possible service in your present work. If you should decide to change jobs later, you will be in a far better position to do so.

Get into the habit of doing more than you are paid for. One day you will be paid for more than you do. If you arrive at work early, stay late, and do a lot in between, you are sure to gain promotion. If you don't receive one, then what? Wait a reasonable time, perhaps a year, and then talk to your immediate superior. Try to find out what the future may hold in the way of opportunities.

If you do not receive encouragement, then and only then would it be wise to explore the possibilities of finding other work.

If yours is a selling job—give more and better service. You will receive in direct proportion to the amount of service you render. If you want more, serve more!

Money will come to you on a sound basis and in large amounts in only one way. The formula? Service—success—then money.

Lasting success is a gradual process. It must begin with service; it can begin in no other way.

Unfortunately, most people want money first. They would like to have everything on a silver platter, and they want it *today*. But that is like asking a stove to produce heat before fuel is provided. It just can't happen—without the fuel, there will be no heat.

So it is with money. If we really want it, we must first give service. There is no question about it, people who give real service enjoy success, and money showers down on successful people in great abundance. This is long-range rather than short-range.

The short-range viewpoint, typified by the man who wants his money today for yet unrendered future services, is fatal. The man thinking in this shortsighted fashion usually ends up with nothing.

Some good friends of mine are attorneys. They have paid a great price for the privilege of practicing law. Years of education, training, and expense were involved before they could hang out their shingles. Then five or ten years more were required for their practices to be built to the point where they were well rewarded financially.

Think of the tremendous price a medical doctor pays for success. He, too, has years of education, training, and expense before he can establish a practice. About five years is average for building his practice to a satisfactory level where he enjoys financial freedom.

There is a price to be paid for success by every professional man. In addition to the long years of preparation, there must be dedication to service.

The price is no different no matter what your occupation may be. If you sincerely want to earn a lot of money, you must be prepared to pay the price—service. If you enthusiastically provide a worthwhile service, you will be richly rewarded and there is no way to stop your rewards. Your rewards may come to you in the most unexpected way or from a surprising source. But they will come. Serve and succeed! Remember this basic rule, and you will be a lasting success: Service—success—then money!

I know and have met people who are not motivated by money. I happen to be one of them, so I know something of the problem they face when striving for a more affluent life. When I was strictly in sales work, I found that money goals would not motivate me to go out and make sales. I was motivated enough by money to want to live comfortably and pay my bills, but not enough to make me want to go the extra mile and earn $100,000 per year.

Because I wasn't motivated by money alone, I was forced to establish much larger and much more worthwhile goals in life than just making sales or just making money. So I established big, far-reaching goals that were worthwhile and designed to help others. Each of these goals created a need for money I must earn for the goals to become reality. This book should be a living testimonial regarding the power of goal setting and planning, for it has been one of my long-range goals.

Only small minds are motivated by "just making sales." Large minds must be motivated by bigger and more worthwhile goals. Once goals have been established, then sales will be the tool used to make them become reality. So if you are not motivated by money, create goals that take money to accomplish. They will motivate you to be highly successful.

> *I bargained with Life for a penny,*
> *And Life would pay no more,*
> *However I begged at evening*
> *When I counted my scanty store.*
> *For Life is a just employer—*
> *He gives you what you ask;*

But once you have set the wages,
Why, you must bear the task.
I worked for a menial's hire,
Only to learn, dismayed,
That any wage I had asked of Life,
Life would have willingly paid.

Money alone does not bring happiness, but you can't be happy without it—balance is the key.

Before going on to the next chapter you must accept the following principles:

1. *True happiness can be achieved only by living a balanced life.*
2. *To be both happy and successful, you must plan in the four major areas of your life: Spiritual—Financial—Educational—Recreational.*
3. *God loves a cheerful giver.*
4. *Serve and succeed!*

Accepting these principles takes you another step closer to a life of happiness and prosperity.

Key Points to Commit to Memory

- When man's eyes are on the Creator, his life will flow with milk and honey!
- Most people simply don't understand that they cannot have both money and things.
- If you can't live on $500 per month—you can't live on $5,000 per month.
- The Bible does not say that money is evil.
- It takes money to accomplish just about anything worthwhile in life.
- No man can attain riches unless he enriches others.
- You can't outgive the Giver!

- Get in the habit of doing more than you are paid for. One day you will be paid for more than you do.
- Service—success—then money!
- Lasting success is a gradual process.
- Money alone does not bring happiness, but you can't be happy without it—balance is the key.

6

Life's Tightrope: Educational and Recreational Balance

Areas Three and Four

It may seem to you that having discussed the importance of the first two areas for true happiness—spiritual and financial—that little else is required to be truly happy. To attain a true balance in life, two additional areas are essential.

The third area is educational and if this is not in harmony with the other principles, your journey toward happiness will be erratic, if not impossible. The fourth area—recreational—meets the needs expressed in the old saying—"All work and no play makes Jack a dull boy." All work will make plenty of "jack" for a short time. After that, poor Jack will be ready for the hospital or a scrap heap. Without relaxation—in satisfactory balance—Jack is headed for a breakdown and you never find true happiness in the conditions surrounding a breakdown.

Area Three: Educational Balance

Have you ever known an individual who was educationally out of balance? He has become so obsessed with gaining knowledge that he becomes an educated fool. He is so technical in his thinking that he forgets how to apply his knowledge in practical situations. His only interest is gaining more and more education, but he never seems to find a way to use knowledge to benefit him and his family. He represents an educated financial tragedy and unfortunately, the world has many people like him. I know men who could paper the south wall of Madison Square Garden with their diplomas and certificates, but they are starving to death. Knowledge without application is useless. Education does not guarantee success, only the application of education will do that.

Then there is the individual who is illiterate. He possesses little or no education. Due to his lack of desire to educate himself, he and his family must suffer the consequences of insufficient education throughout their lives.

Both extremes illustrate educational imbalance. Somewhere between these two extremes, there is a place of perfect educational balance. You arrive at this point through goal setting and planning in the educational area.

There are two kinds of knowledge: general and specialized. Generalized knowledge can help you become a more well-rounded person but it does not necessarily help you earn your living. I have known men who had great knowledge on many subjects, and yet were complete failures in their work. They cluttered their minds with so much that was unimportant that no room was left for the information they needed to earn their living. The knowledge that will guide you in your work and form the foundation for setting goals and establishing plans is called specialized knowledge. If you are a person of normal intelligence, having the willingness to work and the desire to obtain specialized knowledge, you can succeed!

Bill Roberts sells power tools. That's not all he does. Bill, according to his wife, eats and sleeps power tools, too. She may be exaggerating but Bill does spend his spare time keeping up with his business.

When a competitive line brought out a table saw several dollars under his price, he was concerned, but not for long. To achieve the price and to maintain a profit, the competitor had used bearings and other parts that made their saw not truly competitive with his saw.

Bill lost a sale to an old customer a few days after the new model came out. He did his best to persuade his customer to buy his brand but the price difference outweighed his statements about the inability of the new tool to stand up under constant use. When the tool burned out a bearing and overheated with use, the customer returned to the salesman who not only knew his own products but those of his competitors as well.

A salesman who knows only his own products has knowledge, but a salesman who knows his competitors' products as well has specialized knowledge in his field. Too many salesmen, unfortunately, lack even adequate knowledge of the products they sell. Without this knowledge, they must fail; without specialized knowledge, a salesman will not progress to the top. You can obtain this specialized knowledge through experience and study, just as Bill Roberts did.

Each of us should engage in at least one organized educational activity every year. This educational experience will prevent our minds from becoming stagnant and unproductive and will serve to keep us mentally alert, so that we may perform at peak efficiency. You can do this in several different ways—through formal classroom programs, correspondence courses, or individual study. No matter which you choose, do it on a planned basis and for the purpose of gaining specialized knowledge. If possible, persuade a congenial associate to study with you. You will find that two heads can study better than one. Remember, "If you are a person of normal intelligence, having the willingness to work and the desire to obtain specialized knowledge, you can succeed!"

Area Four: Recreational Balance

Have you ever known someone with a recreational imbalance in his life? There are two types, the first "recreates" himself right into financial disaster. His recreational activity dominates his life. He wants to play all of the time, never giving enough attention to the spiritual, financial, and educational areas of his life. This imbalance causes him to be an unhappy and frustrated person, who never finds fulfillment in life.

I have a close friend, Charles E. Pack, of Waco, Texas, who at one time had a recreational imbalance in his life. He is one of the most talented and versatile men that I have ever met. Charlie can do everything! He was an outstanding athlete in high school and college; he is a gifted musician; he is a par golfer; he is a champion bass fisherman; he can beat you at anything you want to do—anything from marbles to chess.

Having ability in such abundance created a problem for Charlie because his life's activity centered around his recreational pursuits, leaving the spiritual, financial, and educational areas to suffer. He was out of balance recreationally!

Charlie came to me several years ago. He said, "Glenn, I have been in the life insurance business for six years and I am worse off today than I was my first day in the field. I am either going to get in or out of the life insurance business! Can you help me?"

I replied, "Charlie, since you ask for help—I will help you." Although I had tried to help him before, he could never hear me.

Jesus said, "He that hath an ear, let him hear!" Each of us has ears, but very few of us can actually hear and understand the truth when it is presented. Usually a man must hit "rock bottom" before his mind is conditioned and receptive to hearing the solutions to his problems.

To make a long, long story short—Charlie heard! Man, did he hear! We went into a three-day goals and planning session behind the closed doors of my office. From that time forward, Charles E. Pack has been a man with a mission in life, destined to be one of the great life insurance salesmen of our time.

Balance did it! Through the goals and planning sessions, all areas of Charlie's life were put into their proper perspective—putting balance into his life. As a follow up to the initial thrust, we met weekly for a "truth session" as Charlie called it. The purpose of this session was to keep him on the track!

Today Charlie Pack is a champion life insurance salesman, and all he did to change his life for the better was apply the Bland Method of Goal Setting and Planning, which was still only an idea within the confines of my mind. Now, the method is being passed on to you. What will you do with it?

As Charlie progressed, he wrote an article for his company's monthly sales publication. The article received such wide acceptance that the Life Insurance Agency Management Association of Hartford, Connecticut, asked permission to print it in their publication,

Management Plans. Here is a portion of the original article. I hope that it will have a message for you.

Knowing many people in this area was a definite asset to me, and a while back I recall a friend of mine introducing me to a stranger with these words, "Mr. Jones, I would like you to meet one of the best bass fishermen in Waco." I believe it was at this point that the sun started coming through. I wondered why my friend didn't mention that I was in the insurance business. I didn't have to wonder very long because I really knew why. At fishing I was a winner; I was not a winner at life insurance.

The real question for me to answer was why I was a winner at fishing and not at life insurance selling. Again, the answer was relatively simple. I had the best fishing rig and rods and reels anyone could buy. And when I went fishing, I thought of nothing but fishing. It's funny how lucky a person gets at fishing or anything else when he eats and sleeps and thinks of nothing but.

Last May 13 I decided to start applying the rules to my business life that I had set for myself when fishing.

The way I work now is that I wake up at 7 A.M. and I'm at the office by 8 A.M. Every Monday morning I have a "truth session," which is analyzing the mistakes I made the week before and gaining new ideas for the week ahead. And I am using the daily planner every day now, even on my afternoon off. I even use reverse psychology in that I plan my work by a month and a year by first taking out my days off. For example, I take out Thursday afternoons, Saturdays, and Sundays. When I do this, it becomes quite logical to me that if I take two and a half days off, I am indeed obligated to work hard the other four and a half days. And there's nothing wrong with working hard. In fact, it is the only way you can achieve goals and gain self-pride. By working the days that I work, I'm gaining for myself (1) professional stature, (2) prestige with my clients, (3) no feelings of guilt when I take time off.

I have sold myself on the idea that four and a half days out of seven isn't bad. And in short time I have even reached the point no one asks me to fish now except on Thursday afternoons and weekends.

I send thank-you letters after every appointment, and I am always looking for new ideas. Of course, I'm only applying many of the ideas and good sales material that I have been taught over the last six years. My point is that the equipment has been there for a long time but it's been lying dormant.

I believe that the key to my change is that I, Charlie Pack, decided to listen and to start trying to do the things that have made other people successful. The more I write, the easier this fishing trip is getting. This is the way it is. I used to think that winning meant to beat somebody or to have someone else say to you, "Charlie, you're great." But I think now that the real definition of winning is *when you tell yourself you are a winner, and believe it!*

I want to thank Charles E. Pack for granting me permission to tell this story. He did it because he wants to help you! There are two basic principles that you should have received from the story of now multimillion-dollar life insurance salesman, Charlie Pack:

1. Imbalance produces unhappiness and frustration, and,
2. The Bland Method of Goal Setting and Planning really works.

Let's look at the second type of recreational imbalance. This man is the exact opposite of Charlie Pack; he enjoys no recreational pleasures at all. He keeps his nose to the grindstone, never having enough time for such "foolish" things as physical exercise and relaxation. He also creates an atmosphere for serious problems in his life.

Every community has its Old Man Tom. As I describe him, you probably will think I am talking about someone you know. Old Man Tom is not old—in years—but he is in his ways.

The place he works just couldn't get along without Old Man Tom. He works early and late. He won't take a vacation. A holiday will find him spending half the day on the job. He takes the job home, too. Tom's wife listens to it on the daily rerun. In the morning he's grumbling about the problems he faces while he eats his breakfast.

No wonder they call him Old Man. He is old—set in his ways—mastered by his job. He is old physically, too, because he never does anything but work or sit and think about it. The last time he had any exercise was when he jumped to a conclusion.

That business will run without Tom one day and probably before long. Adequate recreation would prolong his life, add happiness to his life and, believe it or not, he would be far more valuable to the business.

These two extreme cases point up the need for the ideal situation, perfect balance. Planned recreation is very important to our physical and mental well-being. A strong body and a sound mind must function in complete harmony for success!

In chapters five and six you have been given many of the basic principles of the goal setting and planning process. A balanced life is so important that you should reread these chapters from time to time to keep these principles foremost in your mind. The Bible says, "Any enterprise is built by wise planning, becomes strong through common sense, and profits wonderfully by keeping abreast of the facts" (Proverbs 24:3, 4).

Definite goals and plans are important to you as an individual, but they are equally important to your entire family. Setting definite family goals and establishing definite plans for their fulfillment is a tremendous positive force. You will find more detailed information concerning family planning in the Plan of Action section.

For the time being, remember that you must choose a worthwhile goal and then release yourself from your old self and go to that goal! You see, no one can stop a man with a plan, because no one has a plan to stop him. If you can *believe* what you have read to this point, all things are possible to you—believe and succeed!

Before going on to the next chapter, you must accept the following principles:

1. *Educational and recreational balance is essential to your happiness and success.*
2. *Imbalance produces unhappiness and frustration.*
3. *Set definite goals and plans for the entire family.*

Accepting these principles takes you another step closer to a life of happiness and prosperity.

Key Points to Commit to Memory

- Knowledge without application is useless.
- If you are a person of normal intelligence, having the willingness to work and the desire to obtain specialized knowledge, you can succeed!
- Choose a worthwhile goal and then release yourself from your old self and go to that goal!
- A strong body and a sound mind must function in complete harmony for success!
- No one can stop a man with a plan, because no one has a plan to stop him.
- Believe and succeed!

7

Thirty Golden Minutes

We live in a very complex world! No longer does a man rise before daybreak, milk the cows and gather the eggs, and still have time left to observe the beautiful sunrise. The man who lived this sort of life had abundant opportunity to stay in tune with the world around him. He was constantly reminded by Mother Nature of the never-failing natural laws provided by the Creator. He saw evidence of these overwhelming powers in the birth of a baby calf, the hatching of an egg, and the growth of a stalk of corn. He heard the birds sing and the crickets chirp. He saw wild geese flying south for the winter and squirrels gathering nuts before the snows came. His faith was related to what he saw and experienced every day. He had peace of mind and time to think. His environment created it for him.

Now, in contrast, let's take a quick look at twentieth-century man. He sleeps as late as possible and gulps a cup of coffee on his way to work. He dodges through the morning traffic, honking his horn, cussing out other drivers, stopping for red lights, and squealing his tires to be out front so he will have no trouble getting to the proper lane to make his next turn. He arrives at work, looks for a parking space, waits for an elevator, and finally he is at his desk ready for the opportunities of the day. What sort of frame of mind do you suppose Mr. Twentieth-Century Man is in? I would suspect that it would not be positive and peaceful.

As we have progressed, we have left behind the peace and serenity we once enjoyed. Our modern environment does not automatically create the wholesome atmosphere for slowing down. Consequently, we miss the miraculous blessings which are ours for the taking as they always have been. There are probably some individuals living in New York City who have never seen green grass—their world is one of concrete and steel.

Regardless of where you may live or work, I want to teach you how to get the most out of living your life. You can help to accomplish this by setting aside thirty minutes each morning when you can be completely alone for what I call the Faith Period. Thomas A. Edison said, "To do much clear thinking, a man must arrange for regular periods of solitude when he can concentrate and indulge his imagination without distraction."

The Faith Period is a very important part of the total goal setting and planning procedure—without faith no goal or plan would ever become reality. Since the Faith Period occupies such an important place in the Bland Method of Goal Setting and Planning, we should pause to define the word *faith*. The Bible says, "What is faith? It is the confident assurance that something we want is going to happen. It is the certainty that what we hope for is waiting for us, even though we cannot see it up ahead" (Hebrews 11:1). Faith is what you have left after everything else has been lost. It is the most powerful motivating force in the world. Millions of people are looking to the future with great expectancy because of their faith. Wish and hope, devoid of faith and belief, are fruitless.

The teachings of Jesus Christ were based on faith and belief. He pointed out that faith is the tremendous force that can make good things happen in your life. He also pointed out that most of us possess too little faith. He said, "For if you had faith even as small as a tiny mustard seed, you could say to this mountain, 'Move!' and it would go far away. Nothing would be impossible." With this statement he put most of us into our rightful place. Have you ever seen a mustard seed? Do you realize how small it is? A mustard seed is so tiny that you could put several hundred of them in a teaspoon. Just think, if we can only develop our faith to the smallest degree, we will be able to accomplish fantastic things.

This is what the Faith Period is all about. Its sole purpose is to help you grow in faith which, in turn, will enable you to do outstanding things. Let's get into the actual mechanics of how to conduct your own personal Faith Period. This is a vital part of the goals and planning program which you must fit routinely into your daily activity.

The Faith Period should be a very personal thing! Its purpose is to put you in tune with the great, infinite, intelligent God of the universe. In him lie hidden all the mighty, untapped treasures of wisdom and knowledge. The Faith Period will give you great inspiration— and remember, nothing great was ever accomplished without inspiration!

First, you must form the habit of becoming an early riser. There was a time in my life when I would set my alarm clock to sound just thirty minutes before I was required to be on my job. I would awaken—rush, rush, rush, and then arrive at my work totally and mentally unprepared to meet the opportunities and frustrations of the day. The early morning hours set the stage for the activities of the day. If they are pleasant, the entire day will be pleasant.

Today, I arise each morning at 5:30 and slowly begin to prepare myself for the day. As the shower's warm, relaxing water flows over my body, I have formed the habit of thinking good thoughts. I am very thankful for just being alive and having the opportunity to serve my fellow man. I am thankful for my good friends and business associates. I am thankful for the abundant life I live. I look forward to the day with the great expectancy that good things are going to happen. I slowly eat a moderate breakfast and then drive to the office, arriving at 6:30. Going to the office at this hour of the day creates within you a tremendous feeling of power and authority. At that time of the day you are probably the only person going to work because you want to. The others that you see are going to work because they have to. There's a difference!

The beauty and peace of the early morning hours become a part of you. You literally feel that you are out in front of everyone else, and you are! You feel that the world is yours for the taking. It is! You feel that you can conquer any obstacle standing between you and your goal. You will! By developing the habit of becoming an early riser you have the same advantage in life that a champion sprinter would have if permitted to start the one-hundred-yard dash ten yards ahead of his opponents. He is out in front in the start and through maximum effort, he will stay out front and win the race. The Bible says, "If you love sleep, you will end in poverty. Stay awake, work hard, and there will be plenty to eat!" (Proverbs 20:13).

Another important point is that I have formed the

habit of complimenting those with whom I come in contact in the early morning hours. The compliments give others a tremendous boost for the day, but I benefit most of all because passing the compliments gives me inner happiness. I have a pleasant visit with everyone that I can on my way to the office—the service station attendant who fills my gasoline tank, the building maintenance men, the elevator operator—they are all very important people and I sincerely try to put some extra joy and happiness into their lives. Do you realize that I just might be the only person who gives them a kind word during the entire day? Resolve now to arise early, take your time, and be a cheerful friend, and as a result, you will have many friends.

You are probably thinking, "Man, there ain't no way that I can rise early and be a cheerful friend. I'm a late sleeper!" Let me give you some consolation. I once felt the same way. Learning to rise early involves forming a new habit and there is a price to be paid in the beginning, but once you form the habit, you will wonder how you ever lived any other way. You will discover that your early morning time and your Faith Period will be your most enjoyable and important time of the day.

In the early morning hours your mind is rested and free to soar because it has just awakened from a good night's sleep. It is not crammed with one thousand trivial details that fill it at the end of the day. You can do your most productive thinking in the morning. Become an early riser no matter what your present sleep habits may be.

When I arrive at my office at 6:30 A.M. I immediately begin my Faith Period. I close the office door and light only one lamp so that I may have complete privacy and a soft, warm atmosphere for meditation. Once the stage is set, I begin as follows:

I sit down in a comfortable chair, lean my head back and direct my thoughts toward totally relaxing my entire body. Total relaxation of the physical body frees the mind for deep meditation. Through my thoughts I talk to every part of my body, beginning with my toes:

My toes are completely relaxed;
My feet are completely relaxed;
My legs are completely relaxed;
My hips are completely relaxed;
My stomach is completely relaxed;
My chest is completely relaxed;
My heart is completely relaxed;
My hands are completely relaxed;
My arms are completely relaxed;
My neck is completely relaxed;
My face is completely relaxed;
My mind is completely relaxed;

My total body is now completely relaxed and ready to meditate—totally relaxed.

When my body reaches the point of total relaxation, I read the following meditation:

"Slow me down, O Creator!
Ease the pounding of my heart
By the quieting of my mind.
Steady my hurried pace
With a vision of the eternal reach of time.
Give me,
Amidst the confusion of my day,
The calmness of the everlasting hills.
Break the tensions of my nerves
With the soothing music of the singing streams
That live in my memory.
Help me to know
The magic restoring power of sleep.

Teach me the art
Of taking minute vacations of slowing down
*   to look at a flower;*
*   to chat with an old friend;*
*   or make a new one;*
*   to pet a stray dog;*
*   to watch a spider build a web;*
*   to smile at a child;*
*   or to read a few lines*
*   from a good book.*
Remind me each day
That the race is not always to the swift;
That there is more to life than increasing its speed.
Let me look upward
Into the branches of the towering oak
And know that it grew great and strong
Because it grew slowly and well.
Slow me down, O Creator,
And inspire me to send my roots deep
Into the soil of life's enduring values
That I may grow toward the stars
Of my greater destiny."

At this point my mind is totally prepared to accept inspired thoughts. The preceding meditation should be committed to memory through daily repetition. I continue my Faith Period by reading the 91st Psalm from *The Living Bible:*

We live within the shadow of the Almighty, sheltered by the God who is above all gods.

This I declare, that he alone is my refuge, my place of safety; he is my God, and I am trusting him. For he rescues you from every trap, and protects you from the fatal plague. He will shield you with his wings! They will shelter you. His faithful promises are your armor. Now you don't need to be afraid of the dark any more, nor fear the dangers of the day; nor dread the plagues of darkness, nor disasters in the morning.

Though a thousand fall at my side, though ten thousand are dying around me, the evil will not touch me. I will see how the wicked are punished but I will not share it. For Jehovah is my refuge! I choose the God above all gods to shelter me. How then can evil overtake me or any plague come near? For he orders his angels to protect you wherever you go. They will steady you with their hands to keep you from stumbling against the rocks on the trail. You can safely meet a lion or step on poisonous snakes, yes, even trample them beneath your feet!

For the Lord says, "Because he loves me, I will rescue him; I will make him great because he trusts in my name. When he calls on me I will answer; I will be with him in trouble, and rescue him and honor him. I will satisfy him with a full life and give him my salvation."

You should not put your faith in man. Man will fail you because he is imperfect by nature. Those you love will let you down because they are only human beings and are incapable of having perfect understanding and perfect love. Man will disappoint you time and time again. Many individuals with whom I have had occasion to talk and who have gone down the wrong pathway in life, did so because they felt they had been wronged by someone. So don't put your faith in man, he will hurt you. Put faith in God and his promises, and you will have the strength to withstand any adversity!

Put your faith in the principles and they will sustain you.

Emerson once very wisely said, "Alone, a man is sincere; upon the approach of another, then hypocrisy begins." The Faith Period is a time when you have opportunity to be sincere with yourself. A man needs to have his moment to be alone with his Creator daily. It helps him to keep the proper perspective about life.

As I continue my Faith Period, I communicate to God through my thoughts. People have asked me, "How do you do that? And here is the answer that I have given them and also the procedure I use in my own life. I imagine that the Creator is sitting in a chair in the room with me. I imagine that he is the very best friend that I have ever had and then, I just simply talk to him through my thoughts. I imagine that he is not only the best and most loyal friend that I have ever had, but also the wisest. He has all of the answers. I use the following procedure when talking with him:

• The Creator is the one who forgives. There is no reason for man to carry the burden of his mistakes around on his shoulders all of his life. If I have made any mistakes that can be recalled, I discuss them with him, asking him to lift the burden from me—he does! Once this is done, my mind is free to work and create. The forgiving of your mistakes in life has been provided for in the Creator's plan.

• Next, I give thanks for all of the good things that happened to me the previous day.

• Then my thoughts turn to the interests of others. I express my concern for those I love, those in need, the sick—and for those I resent. It is a proven fact that your own attitude improves greatly when you are considerate of the needs of others.

• Next, my thoughts turn to my own personal needs,

both problems and opportunities. Through my thoughts I petition for answers and results, claiming the promise that is mine; "Listen to me! You can pray for anything, and if you believe, you have it; it's yours!" (Mark 11:24). We are also given the promise, "Ask, and you will be given what you ask for. Seek and you will find. Knock, and the door will be opened. For everyone who asks, receives. Anyone who seeks, finds. If only you will knock, the door will be opened" (Matthew 7:7, 8).

You Must Expect a Miracle!

After the meditation portion of the Faith Period has ended, the time has come to program your mind by repetition of your goals and plans. If you will keep your goals before you each day, they are certain to become reality. How can you do this? It can be developed by voluntarily repeating orders from your thinking mind to your subconscious mind for the purpose in which you want to develop faith. Your conscious mind can program your subconscious mind; and the subconscious mind will convert thoughts into reality. You program the subconscious mind by continuously repeating the information you feed into it. Repetition indelibly engraves your conscious thoughts upon the subconscious mind. Understanding your subconscious mind is vitally important if you are to be successful at goal setting and planning.

Your subconscious mind can be compared to very fertile farm land. The soil does not care what is planted in it. That choice is left up to the farmer. The land will only take what is planted, make it grow and then return it to you in great abundance. Remember, your subconscious does not care what you plant. That is strictly up to you. You can plant good or you can plant evil. Either will grow equally well.

The subconscious mind cannot choose. It can only act upon the information that it receives. Your physical body and conscious mind must sleep to replenish their energy, but the subconscious mind never sleeps. It is on the job twenty-four hours a day. The subconscious mind is the connecting link between a person's thinking mind and the great store of accumulated knowledge and experience available to all people. And what of those situations when human wisdom and good intentions are not enough—when one comes to the end of his own resources for problem-solving? It is then that the person in tune with the great Creator-God can draw confidently on the infinite resources promised in James 1:5: "If you want to know what God wants you to do, ask him, and he will gladly tell you, for he is always ready to give a bountiful supply of wisdom to all who ask him; he will not resent it." You may receive the answer when you least expect it. You may be tying your shoe, taking a walk or driving your car when the answer hits you like lightning! When the answer finally comes, it is so clear and simple that you wonder why you never thought of it before.

That is the way that the subconscious works and I will not go into a detailed explanation as to why. It is not my objective to teach you how to build a watch, I want only to teach you how to tell time. I will teach you to program your subconscious mind through procedures that will be applied during the Faith Period, as well as several other times during the day.

At this point, read through your Plan of Action section. Next glance through your Monthly Activity Planner, then check your Weekly Activity Planner to be sure that all top priority items and details have been written down. The next step is to transfer the plans from the Weekly Activity Planner to the Daily Activity Planner and then take action—make it happen!

One other thing that you must do to be successful at goal setting and planning is use a Faith Card. Instructions on how to make your own personal Faith Card can be found in the back of the Plan of Action section. The Faith Card should be carried at all times and read three times each day—just before breakfast, lunch, and then just before going to sleep at night. Also, you will find instructions regarding how to make a Visualization Board to help keep your goals before you each day.

You have been given a detailed example of how I personally conduct my own Faith Period. This example will help you design one for yourself. Take thirty minutes of your time and find a place where you can be alone each morning and follow an established procedure. If you do, your life will immediately be changed for the better and within a ten to thirty-day period you will experience some remarkably good things happening to you. Without it, you will most likely never even begin to reach your full potential as a happy and successful person, living a balanced life. Life is nothing more than opportunity and the Faith Period will help you take full advantage of it. You must quit thinking about the things you fear, and have faith! "I will instruct you [says the Lord] and guide you along the best pathway for your life; I will advise you and watch your progress" (Psalm 32:8). You can do it if you have faith!

Before going on to the next chapter, you must accept the following principles:

1. *You need Thirty Golden Minutes each morning to meditate, plan, and organize your activities for the day.*
2. *You must develop an organized procedure for conducting your Faith Period.*

3. *As your faith increases, your deeds will grow.*
4. *Through the Faith Period you can program your mind for happiness and success.*

Accepting these principles takes you another step closer to a life of happiness and prosperity.

Key Points to Commit to Memory

- Without faith, no goal or plan would ever become reality.
- Faith is what you have left after everything else has been lost.
- Wish and hope, devoid of faith and belief, are fruitless.
- Nothing great was ever accomplished without inspiration!
- The early morning hours set the stage for the activities of the day.
- Put your faith in the Creator and his promises and you will have the strength to withstand any adversity!
- If you will keep your goals before you each day, they are certain to become reality.
- Repetition indelibly engraves your conscious thoughts upon the subconscious mind.
- All the resources of the knowledge and experience of man and the wisdom of God are available to those in tune with the Creator.
- Life is nothing more than an opportunity and the Faith Period will help you take full advantage of it.
- You must quit thinking about the things you fear and have faith!
- You can do it if you have *faith!*

8

A Priceless Commodity— Yours for the Taking

The man who is the master of human relations is priceless! He is in demand! Opportunity is searching for the man who can turn others on. Industry and business will richly reward the individual who can expertly achieve positive results through other people. The world of private business seeks constantly for that special person who possesses that extraordinary talent of making customers want to go out of their way just to do business with him. The sales field provides fantastic earning potential for the "go getter" who sincerely likes people and can achieve positive results by working through them. Yes, being a master of human relations will open many doors to unlimited opportunity.

Despite the tremendous opportunities, how many people do you know who have developed this tremendous skill? Very few!

I have had the good fortune and pleasure to work side by side with many people from every walk of life. I have been seated at the huge oak conference tables in the smoke-filled board rooms of some of America's most successful corporations and have helped lay plans to earn millions of dollars of new profits. But on the other side of the fence, I can also remember laying miles and miles of pipeline across the desert country of Texas while working in 115-degree heat.

But, in all of my experience, I don't believe that I have met more than a handful of men whom I would consider masters of the art of human relations. I have found without exception that men who possess this outstanding skill are men who are on their way to the top, or men who have already reached the pinnacle of success.

Why are men who master human relations so successful? Why are they so well liked and accepted by others? Why does good fortune seem to smile upon them at every turn? It is because they have learned and accepted a rule, a simple principle that is the key to relating to your fellow man. Some call it the Golden Rule. *"Do for others what you want them to do for you."*

By enthusiastically applying the Golden Rule in your own life, you will enrich the lives of many others, but by far the greater reward will come to you. For every action, there will be a reaction! If the action is good, the reaction will be good. But, on the other hand, if the action is bad, the reaction will be bad.

Applying this great principle will cause good to be radiated from you. In turn, good will be returned to you in the form of happiness and prosperity. The people with whom you come in contact will suddenly become members of your fan club. They will want to play ball on your team, which will eventually push you right to the top. Treating others as you like them to treat you will cause them to do everything within their power to help you achieve your goals in life.

You may meet someone who will not respond to this rule. If so, go the extra mile with him, showing him patience and understanding. Treat him exactly like the person you want him to be and he will do his very best to become that person. You will find this principle to be very effective in dealing with your superiors. I have seen this principle change tyrannical and uncooperative corporate presidents to soft-spoken lambs who could not do enough for you. Let me repeat this principle: "If you treat a person like the person you want him to be, he will do his best to become that person"—try it, it works!

Now let's examine a master of the art of human relations. This man is a leader of men. He is happy. He is very prosperous. He is everything that you could conceivably want to be. Let's take a look at his inner being and how he relates to others. Let's attempt to discover why he is so unbelievably successful at making people like him. Project yourself into his shoes and see if they fit.

The Portrait of a Master of Human Relations

1. *He will seem simple, but be wise.* The French author Montesquieu said, "I have always observed that to succeed in the world, a man must seem simple, but be wise." If you appear to be a simple man, others will tend to underestimate your ability, and will present you the opportunity to deal with them when their guard is down. If you were known to be a man of many words who possessed a sharp wit, others would automatically prepare a defense for the mental assault they are expecting from you. By seeming simple, but being wise, you can literally accomplish your objectives before anyone actually realizes what has happened and yet, everyone will be happy.

You have seen those men rise to the top who suffer from egomania and are full of arrogance and conceit.

They are not loved and admired by their associates and will be trampled under foot at the first opportunity. Their days are numbered! King David said, "I myself have seen it happen: a proud and evil man, towering like a cedar of Lebanon, but when I looked again, he was gone! I searched for him but could not find him! But the good man—what a different story! For the good man—the blameless, the upright, the man of peace—he has a wonderful future ahead of him. For him there is a happy ending. But evil men shall be destroyed and their posterity shall be cut off" (Psalm 37:35-38). Regardless of how discouraging it may seem at times, right will always prevail in the end; it is a natural law. "The wicked will finally lose; the righteous will finally win" (Proverbs 21:18).

2. *He will be humble.* He will not be all puffed up with pride to the point of offending others. He will be able to accept his great achievements for their true worth and not as something that makes him better than the next person. He will possess a consistent control over his temper because a quick, ill temper affects his judgment and relations with others. The Good Shepherd said, "For everyone who tries to honor himself shall be humbled; and he who humbles himself shall be honored" (Luke 14:11). One of the definite characteristics of a man who has mastered the art of human relations is humility, a characteristic that everyone respects.

3. *He will be genuinely interested in his fellow man.* He will treat each individual with great respect regardless of his social status. Every individual is important to him because he knows that every man is a child of God and has a useful service to render to mankind. He is a man that you can talk with and share your innermost

secrets. He will take time to listen and he is able to offer you sound advice. He has the capacity to sincerely love his brother. He has empathy. "Don't just pretend that you love others; really love them. Hate what is wrong. Stand on the side of good. Love each other with brotherly affection and take delight in honoring each other" (Romans 12:9, 10).

4. *He will be honest and truthful in all of his business dealings and personal life.* To succeed in working with people you must be honest and truthful in every facet of your life. In Romans 12:17 we find this statement, "Do things in such a way that everyone can see you are honest clear through." Leave no room for any doubt! If your friends and business associates consider you to be an honest man, they will entrust to you the big responsibilities regarding business and financial matters. Honesty and truthfulness go hand in hand. You cannot possess one without the other.

God has said, "Here is your part; tell the truth. Be fair. Live at peace with everyone. Don't plot to harm others; don't swear that something is true when it isn't! How I hate all that sort of thing!" (Zechariah 8:16, 17). If you are honest and truthful in all of your dealings with others, you will be richly rewarded. If you learn to handle wisely the pennies of others, you will be given the opportunity to handle their great fortunes. Opportunity comes to the honest and truthful man! "His master praised him for good work. You have been faithful in handling this small amount, he told him, so now I will give you many more responsibilities" (Matthew 25:23).

5. *He will not involve himself in gossip and slander.* He realizes that malicious gossip is spread by people with small minds. "Any story sounds true until some-

one tells the other side and sets the record straight" (Proverbs 18:17). If you must gossip, go to a great ocean and write your slanderous rumors in the sand at the water's edge, so that they will forever be washed away by the incoming tide. Idle gossip destroys others and it will destroy you also if you clutter your mind with it. If you can't say something good about a person—say nothing! You will be much happier and a better person for having done so.

6. *He will give credit and praise to others.* One of the easiest ways to lose the loyalty and support of others is by taking all of the credit for the accomplishment of objectives yourself. Leave yourself out of the picture. Heap all of the praise on others. They, in turn, will give you more praise than you could ever generate for yourself. Give the praise to others and you take the money. "Don't praise yourself; let others do it!" (Proverbs 27:2). This is very difficult, but praise will come to you in great abundance if you truly deserve it.

7. *He will be patient and kind.* You must acquire the ability to be patient. The youthful and inexperienced do not understand the great power of having patience. They tend to want everything to happen yesterday. Recently, I saw a cartoon which reminded me of the one who is impatient with life. Two vultures gazed at each other while sitting on the limb of a dead tree in the middle of the desert. The caption read, "Patience hell, let's kill something!" This seems to be the attitude of many people who do not truly understand the power of patience.

Disraeli said, "Everything comes if a man will only wait. I have brought myself by long meditation to the conviction that a human being with a settled purpose must accomplish it, and nothing can resist a will that will stay in existence for its fulfillment."

Another important virtue that you must possess is kindness. This characteristic will help others to like you and it will also create within your soul an inner peace that can be found no other way. You are the one who really benefits by being kind to others. "Your own soul is nourished when you are kind; it is destroyed when you are cruel" (Proverbs 11:17).

8. *He will be fair and just.* Your business associates and friends can accept almost anything you do if they feel that they are being treated fairly and with justice. People naturally resent unfair treatment. They resent special favors for one individual that are not available to everyone. Showing favoritism destroys the harmony of the entire group—business associates or friends. Their opinion is, "What's good for the goose is good for the gander," and they are right. Present each individual an equal opportunity and then let their own efforts determine how happy and successful they will become. Rewards should be based on results!

A master of human relations must also be just. He must gather all of the facts concerning a situation, consider all of the solutions, then make the best decision based on the facts and stick with it. When a business associate or friend gets off the right track he is obligated to try to prevent this from happening.

I have observed men in high places of authority ignore a friend or business associate who had taken the wrong pathway. They actually refused to help. Their excuse was, "I don't want to get involved." Their attitude was, "Let him hang himself, that's his problem. I have enough of my own." Invariably, the friend who hits rock bottom will always get around to asking, "Why didn't you tell me I was going in the wrong direction?" This is a difficult question to answer!

If you know someone you feel is going in the wrong

direction, you should offer him your assistance and counsel at least once—you owe it to him. You will always be happy you did! If you treat others fairly and with justice they will always hold you in very high regard. "The Lord demands fairness in every business deal. He established this principle" (Proverbs 16:11).

9. *He will give and accept constructive criticism.* If you are in a position requiring you to work through other people to achieve positive results, there will be times when it is necessary to offer constructive criticism. Constructive criticism has only one purpose—to help others. It should never be administered as a rebuke, but only as a means to arrive at solutions for adverse situations which occur to everyone who takes action. The only people who do not create problems are those doing nothing. The rest—the "doers"—must continually face problems each day.

The master of human relations must also be willing to accept constructive criticism. He must be willing to listen to the complaints of those around him, weigh them carefully in his thoughts, extract the truth, and then profit by them. This helps a man grow in his personal life, as well as his work. If you ever get so big that you can no longer take time to listen to constructive criticism, you will not be "big" very long. When it comes from someone you deeply respect, it helps you to remain humble and productive. Welcome it! "Don't refuse to accept criticism: get all the help you can" (Proverbs 23:12).

10. *He will be a decent person.* No man is perfect and everyone makes mistakes, so do not expect your friends and business associates to go through life never making a wave. They will make mistakes and you will make mistakes, because we are all human.

You must strive every day to live within the boundaries of the unwritten laws of the Creator. You will fail from time to time, but when you do—get back on the track. That's the important thing! If you study the life of King David, one of the Creator's most beloved, you will find that he was a rascal. He was continuously getting off the right track, but he was aware of his human weakness and, by admitting his mistakes, put himself back on the correct course. He found great favor with his people and with God.

If others know that you are basically a sound person, they will overlook the mistakes that you have made and focus their attention upon the many good things you stand for. You cannot master the art of human relations if you consistently live an indecent life— others will not respect nor follow you. "The Lord blesses good men" (Proverbs 12:2).

11. *He will be generous with others.* Here we are not referring to the word "generous" in the material sense. We refer to his generosity in offering himself to others. He cannot allow "self" to stand in the way—others come first.

I remember well when I was a head football coach. I was fortunate to have several good assistant coaches working under my direction. Since we were paid for a nine-month school year, it was necessary for all of the coaches to find summer work to supplement their income. I always made certain that my assistant coaches had secured good summer jobs before I began to look for one. This is a simple illustration, but it presents a perfect example of being generous by putting other people's needs first. These coaches were very important to me. I could not have succeeded without their full support and loyalty, so I made sure they were happy. The result—they took such an interest in me that I ended with the very best summer work to be found. They also returned generosity to me many times over in the form of results—winning football games!

Simply forget about getting. Be generous, give of yourself, and good things will happen to you. "And all goes well for the generous man who conducts his business fairly" (Psalm 112:5).

Never fear that your generosity will not be returned to you for it will—it is a natural law. "Give generously, for your gifts will be returned to you later" (Ecclesiastes 11:1).

12. *He will possess a positive mental attitude.* A positive mental attitude is a powerful magnet that will attract others to you just as bees are attracted to honey. Your friends and business associates will just naturally want to be around you if you display a sunny outlook toward the world. What are your first thoughts when you awake each morning? Do you say, "Good morning, God" or "Good God, it's morning"? This illustrates whether you are a positive or negative person. When you look at a half a glass of water, do you say, "The glass is half full" or do you say "The glass is half empty"? Your answer definitely reflects how you view the world around you. You must learn to be optimistic and to live in the expectation that good things are going to happen if you are to be a master of human relations.

You may have heard the story of the little twin brothers, one a pessimist and the other an optimist. The little pessimist was always complaining and very negative, while the optimist viewed everything through rose-colored glasses. It was Christmas, and their father decided to truly test their attitudes. He placed every kind of beautiful toy imaginable under the Christmas tree for the pessimist—a new bike, a basketball, a rifle, and dozens of things that would make a little boy happy. On the other side of the tree, he placed a pile of horse manure, as the only present for the optimist.

Early Christmas morning the father hid behind a sofa to watch. The pessimist entered first and saw all of the beautiful toys with his name on them. He immediately began to complain, "If I take this new bike outside to ride and have a wreck, I might hurt myself and Dad sure would be mad. Oh, there is a basketball. I know that the first time I play with it I am sure to puncture it. Hey, there is a rifle, but I better not play with it because, sure as the world, I'll break a neighbor's window," and he went on and on, deep in negativism. Christmas morning to him was a disaster!

Then, in came the little optimist. When he saw the pile of horse manure with his name on it, he enthusiastically began to run throughout the house looking in all of the rooms, in the garage, and in the backyard. When his father caught him by the arm and asked, "Son, what are you looking for?" the optimist replied, "Dad, with all of the horse manure that I found under the Christmas tree, I just know there's gotta be a pony around here someplace!"

A positive mental attitude plays an important role in human relations—it is contagious and rubs off on others. Remember: Maintain a positive mental attitude and you will go far in dealing with people.

One who possesses all twelve qualities will rise to great heights in this life, and will be long remembered after he returns to the dust from which he came. He is a Master of Human Relations. He will accomplish all of his goals in life by working through other people. He makes them all his partners in every venture and leads them to a productive life of happiness and success. They will follow him through every adversity and enjoy with him every victory. He knows how to work with people. He applies the Golden Rule.

There are several other principles which should be discussed before leaving this chapter on human relations. Understanding the following principles will make your climb up the ladder of happiness and success much less frustrating and will give you much deeper insight into the way things really are.

If you sincerely want to accomplish outstanding things and be happy and successful, you must surround yourself with capable helpers. Some executives refuse to hire subordinates with ability and potential for fear they will eventually take their jobs. But in reality, it works just the opposite! The executive who fears to hire capable people loses his job because of poor results, while the executive who surrounds himself with enthusiastic people of ability is promoted to be president of the company.

You will be no better or no more effective than the people around you. A head football coach is no better than his assistant coaches, and the president of a corporation is no better than his administrative staff. The chief can only set the goals; it takes the Indians to carry them out. Surround yourself with top-notch Indians as you grow toward success—they will make a big man out of you!

Another principle involving human relations that you surely want to remember is that you should never get involved in personalities. As you go to the top there will always be inequities. There will always be the corporate president who promotes his twenty-three-year-old son to vice-president after only six months of service, or the junior executive who pushes his way to the top because of favoritism rather than results. And then there is the flash-in-the-pan salesman who yells the loudest, and therefore gets all of the attention.

There will always be the guy who sleeps on the job, but receives the same raise you do, when you have been doing all the work. There will always be unfairness and injustice to face as long as there are people.

If the people who receive such favoritism do not deserve to be at the top, they will not stay there. I have seen them fall! It is the most pitiful sight when they have to stand on their own without someone to hold their hand and advise them. There are so many enemies made on the way up, waiting to pick them off at the first chance. A worker who is promoted for reasons other than his ability and results will eliminate himself. It is a temporary situation that will solve itself. Don't get involved, keep working toward your own personal goals, and let the vultures pick his bones clean. You must be big enough not to become involved if you really want to go places!

As you become successful you will take others to the top with you. You will blaze new trails and do things that have never been done before, and at that particular time, you may be compensated very little. New men will be started with benefits and with an income that was not available to you when you began. But you can't look back. If you want to progress, don't envy them, for you have something that they will never possess and that is knowledge and know-how, which you obtained by paying the price of hard work. No one can ever take that from you. It is yours to share until the day you die; it is priceless to you, if you will only use it. It will earn you more opportunities than someone who has not paid the price could even dream possible.

You will take others to the top with you, but if they do not deserve to be there, they will not stay! Free yourself from all pettiness and prejudice. Hope that all those you take to the top will find happiness and success. Set your sights on your own personal goals and let no one stand in your way—that's what it's all about! It takes character to keep forging ahead!

In this chapter, I have outlined some simple principles of human relations, which if applied, will enable you to be one of the top salesmen in your company, the most outstanding teacher in your school system, one of the top executives of your corporation, a top personality in show business, or the most successful businessman in your city. It doesn't matter what your vocation may be. The principles will apply—they will work for you—try them! If you master the art of human relations you can achieve anything your heart desires just by working through people. Simply take time to find out what other people want and then spend your time helping them to get it and you will be successful. Again, please remember, "Do for others what you want them to do for you." You can be a master of human relations if you *believe* you can!

Before going on to the next chapter, you must accept the following principles:

1. *Becoming a master of human relations will make you a leader.*
2. *This is a skill that can be developed by putting forth the effort.*
3. *Learn and apply the twelve principles found in this chapter.*

Accepting these principles takes you another step closer to a life of happiness and success.

Key Points to Commit to Memory

- The person who is the master of human relations is priceless!

- For every action, there will be a reaction.
- If you treat a person like the person you want him to be, he will do his best to become that person.
- Surround yourself with capable helpers.
- Never get involved in personalities.
- You will take others to the top with you.
- Find out what other people want, help them to get it and you will be successful.

9

You and Opportunity

You are important! You possess talents that are possessed by no other living creature. You need only to develop your talents—translate them into useful services—then you will be well on your way to a lifetime of happiness and success.

You possess these talents because you are a unique creation. You are the only one of your kind: No other individual has existed in the past, is in existence today, or ever will exist who is the carbon copy of you. It was planned that way by the Creator from the beginning. The useful services that you can render are unique to you. No one else can do it just the way you can. Your talents lie deep in the dark recesses of your heart and it is necessary that they be brought to light before you can find happiness and success.

You must search deep inside yourself and find those talents. Your talents will coordinate perfectly with your wants and desires once you discover them. Only by discovering them will you ever find happiness and success. Once you truly discover your own personal talents and put them to work as a useful service for others, you will be happy and successful, because you will be doing the things that you want to do and those are the things you do best!

Each day lots of people go to work only because they have to. They sit at their desks and go through the motions of doing work they literally hate. They are miserable. My sympathy goes out to them. They are working only to hold their jobs. They are not doing something that they really want to do, therefore they receive no fulfillment. They have let society stick them into a tiny slot and they will remain there until they experience a change of attitude or until they die. Conformity destroys a man's initiative and independence. It suppresses his powerful inner drive to do his own thing.

The great teacher Paul of Tarsus explained it this way: "Don't copy the behavior and customs of this world, but be a new and different person with a fresh newness in all you do and think" (Romans 12:2). The Apostle is saying to us, *"Do not conform"*—dare to be different—do your own thing—as long as you operate within the bounds of the great natural laws of the universe, which were established by our Creator.

You have a spirit within you which will lead you to greatness. Every man possesses this spirit! It is a spirit that can mold your life so you will truly achieve your maximum potential. It is the same spirit that molded a backwoods Illinois farm boy into a great statesman and president. It is the same spirit that inspired a lowly orphan boy to become Babe Ruth, the home-run king. It is the same spirit that encouraged a deaf young man, with little formal education, to become the world's outstanding idea man and inventor. It is the same spirit that prompted General MacArthur to glance over his shoulder as he retreated under a barrage of enemy fire, to utter the immortal words, "I shall return."

It is the same spirit that enabled a little-known country preacher to become a dynamic world-renowned evangelist. It is the same spirit that motivated a young Jewish boy to grow up to become the world's outstanding life insurance salesman. It is the same spirit that directed a man whose only desire was to sell clothing and give good service, to build a financial empire.

They demonstrated *the same spirit that lives within you!* This spirit is available only to those who seek it— it is the spirit of the Creator. It lives within us all, but must be developed. If you will develop this spirit to an advanced degree you will become a leader. You can be great if you *believe* you can!

Regardless of your present circumstances, you can be happy and successful. Happiness and success are attitudes of mind and can be enjoyed by anyone who develops the proper attitude toward life. By taking complete control of your thoughts, you can rise above your negative circumstances.

Throughout history, few people, if any, have suffered greater adversity than Helen Keller. A serious illness, diagnosed as brain fever, destroyed her sight and hearing before she was two years old. Because of this, she was unable to speak and was entirely shut off from the world, living as a deaf-mute. Her teacher, Anne Sullivan, was able to make contact with the young girl's mind through the sense of touch. Within three years, she knew the alphabet, and could read and write in Braille.

Until the age of ten, she could talk only in the sign language of the deaf-mute. She decided she would learn to speak, and by the time she was sixteen, her speech had progressed enough to allow her to enter preparatory school. In 1904 she was graduated from Radcliffe, with honors.

After college, she became a noted lecturer and

author. She lectured on behalf of the blind and deaf-blind in more than twenty-five countries on the five major continents. Her books are best sellers and have been translated into more than fifty languages.

It would have been very easy for Helen Keller to lose her faith and give up all hope many times during her life. But she didn't because she had come to the realization that she was a child of God, that she was a unique creation possessing tremendous potential and that she had within her mind the seed of an important service to render for mankind. Her love and concern for others gained her worldwide fame; actually, she became a legend in her own lifetime.

You probably do not have to overcome as great a degree of adversity as Helen Keller to secure a happy and successful life. You need only to realize, as she did, that outward circumstances do not determine your destiny. Your circumstances can be altered at any time you choose, so that you may begin your journey toward inner peace, riches, enlightenment, and physical well-being. George Bernard Shaw, the Irish dramatist and critic, said, "People are always blaming their circumstances for what they are. I don't believe in circumstances. The people who get on in this world are the people who get up and look for the circumstances they want and if they can't find them—make them!"

Are you allowing your present circumstances to keep you from achieving your full potential as a person? If you are, you are wasting your God-given talents because of your reluctance to make a decision to change your unfavorable circumstances. Why are you reluctant to make such a decision? Probably because of fears, doubts, or excuses that continually saturate your thoughts. William Shakespeare wrote this jewel of wisdom, "Our doubts are traitors and make us lose the good we oft might win, by fearing to attempt." Someone else put it this way: "Even a turtle cannot go anywhere unless he sticks his neck out first."

If you have a genuine thirst for opportunity, then you must launch out confidently, leaving the details of providing for the necessities of life to the spirit within you. Jesus said,

> So my counsel is: don't worry about things— food, drink, and clothes. For you already have life and a body—and they are far more important than what to eat and wear. Look at the birds! They don't worry about what to eat—they don't need to sow or reap or store up food—for your heavenly Father feeds them. And you are far more valuable to him than they are. Will all your worries add a single moment to your life? And why worry about your clothes? Look at the field lilies! They don't worry about theirs. Yet, King Solomon in all his glory was not clothed as beautifully as they. And if God cares so wonderfully for flowers that are here today and gone tomorrow, won't he more surely care for you, O men of little faith?
>
> So don't worry at all about having enough food and clothing. Why be like the heathen? For they take pride in all these things and are deeply concerned about them. But your heavenly Father already knows perfectly well that you need them, and he will give them to you if you give him first place in your life and live as he wants you to (Matthew 6:25-33).

If you have worthwhile goals and are going in the right direction, all of your needs will be provided for.

Commit everything you do to the Lord. Trust him to help you do it and he will (Psalm 37:5). We should make plans—counting on God to direct us (Proverbs 16:9). And it is he who will supply all your needs from his riches in glory (Philippians 4:19).

You can be confident that if you are living within the boundaries of God's guidelines for mankind, he will meet all your needs.

Too many people today feel unloved and unwanted—they feel that nobody really cares about them. They are wrong! The Creator cares for each of us with a perfect love which is beyond human understanding. To him you are very important. To him you are an individual.

Jesus said, "Even the very hairs of your head are numbered." This should give you some idea as to how important you are to him. His love is personal and it will never fail you. He will counsel with you, give you strength and understanding, and then provide you with the solutions to your opportunities and problems. Human love will fail you. The Psalmist instructs, "It is better to trust the Lord than to put confidence in men" (Psalm 118:8). Human love is imperfect, but the love of the Creator is perfect. In him you have a true friend, one who cares about you. If you are his child, his Spirit is within you. When you call upon him, he will be there whether it be for insignificant things or the building of an empire.

Each of us has within him the seed of greatness! If you nourish this seed until it grows into a towering oak of perfection, "All things will be possible to you." The Creator has provided the way for you to be happy and successful, and your only limitation is your degree of development. The closer you grow to perfection, the greater the degree of happiness and success. The more closely you apply the Creator's guidelines for happiness, and success, the greater will be your accomplishment.

If you think that you are not loved—forget it! You are loved so much that a Man gave his life for you. Forget about needing human love, for it is very fragile and can be completely shattered at any time. Seek only the perfect love of the Creator, and, in addition, you will also receive human love.

Within your being, you have the spirit to be happy and successful! You need no other love than the one true love offered in great abundance by the One who really cares the most about you—the Creator of all.

Fully realizing now that you are a unique being with talents and services to offer that are possessed by no other creature, and that you are deeply loved and cared for, it is time to explore the great unwritten universal laws that govern the unlimited opportunities available to you. Let us take inventory and see what the world has to offer the person seeking happiness and success.

Some believe that "opportunity knocks" only for the rich and powerful. Some believe that there is a "fickle finger of fate" that taps certain individuals on the shoulder and points them in the direction of wealth and power.

Some believe that opportunity has passed them by. They don't believe that an individual is rewarded in direct proportion to the thought and effort he puts forth. They often possess the attitude: "What are you going to do for me?" or "What are you going to do to solve my problem?" They do not truly understand that natural law says that they will only get out of life what they put into it. They want someone to help them without doing anything to help themselves. People who think this way could not possibly be further from the truth regarding what it really takes for them to be happy and successful.

Just after graduation from college, two of my young friends asked a multimillionaire about the chance of earning a million dollars. The old gentleman had little formal education, he had only completed the fifth grade, but he possessed a lot of common sense.

My friends said they thought it more difficult to earn $1,000,000 today than ever before, and they gave many reasons to prove their point. Finally, they asked the old gentleman for his opinion. He had waited very patiently for his turn to talk. "I think it is easier to earn a million dollars today than ever before," he said. "You boys have a problem though, that I didn't have when I started out to earn my first million—you went to college! College teaches you a lot of theory and to work for someone else. They don't teach you how to strike out on your own as I did when I was your age."

I have never forgotten his comment, because it is a basic truth. We must break the bonds of conformity and then use all of our mental and physical resources, regardless of where we live, to produce a lifetime of happiness and success.

Observe the tremendous abundance all around you. Nature blossoms forth with unending beauty. Take a walk in the country and see the unlimited way that our Creator has provided for all of the needs of nature. Drive through the heart of your city and consider the fantastic ingenuity and wealth required to construct the skyscrapers and to build the freeway systems. As you observe all the tremendous abundance around you, remember this, you have as much right to that abundance as any other person. You can "stake your claim" on your rightful portion by simply directing your thoughts to that end. But never forget, it will not be given to you, it must be earned—this is nature's compensation plan for those desiring happiness and success.

Opportunity comes to those who seek it. *Webster's New World Dictionary* defines opportunity as "a time or occasion that is right for doing something." The "time or occasion that is right" will appear when you have mentally prepared yourself to recognize and receive it. To bring this opportunity to fruition requires "doing something."

Desiring to be more successful and to provide opportunity for others to succeed as well, two friends living in Michigan, Jay Van Andel and Richard DeVos, developed a unique marketing concept based on the principles of free enterprise. Because they established their goals, made definite plans, and then took action, the Amway Corporation was founded in 1959. As a result, thousands of right-thinking people throughout the world are enjoying the rewards of building their own successful businesses. Opportunity came to Jay and Rich and the thousands of independent Amway business people because they were earnestly seeking it.

One man living in Tennessee took his family to Florida for a vacation. During the trip, he discovered that it was very difficult for travelers to find motel accommodations providing quality service and adequate facilities for the entire family. After returning home, he approached a friend with the idea of starting a new motel chain, placing emphasis on good service with a family atmosphere. They began by building one motel in their hometown, and in little more than one decade, had built an international motel chain, larger than all their competitors combined. Through an unpleasant vacation experience, opportunity presented itself.

A friend, who was formerly an executive with a large fund-raising company, became unhappy with his work due to conflicting business philosophies. He resigned his position and formed his own company with $3,000 of borrowed capital. He established a business philosophy for the new company based on the eternal laws of happiness and success. As a result, the company has experienced phenomenal growth and is rapidly overtaking all of its competitors. Opportunity emerged in this situation due to my friend's unwillingness to sacrifice his principles, even when it meant losing a good job. Demosthenes, the Greek orator and statesman, said, "Small opportunities are often the beginning of great enterprises."

Opportunity is everywhere! An opportunist once observed, "It is where you find it." Opportunity will seek you out many times during your lifetime. Most people don't recognize it for what it is or they allow fear to cripple their thoughts of success.

My father told me a story of a man with whom he worked in the Oklahoma oil fields. The two were sincere friends, and each had great respect for the abilities of the other. They had worked for the same large oil company for a number of years, and were doing very well financially. One day, as if from the blue, the friend told my father that he was resigning from his present job and was going to become an Oklahoma wildcatter. He would borrow money and begin drilling his own oil wells as an independent contractor. He offered my father a partnership if he would be willing to join him in the venture. Knowing the high risk of failure involved in such a venture, my father declined his friend's offer. Today my father is living on the income from his company pension plan, while his friend is enjoying the affluent life of a wealthy oilman. Fear of failure has caused many capable men to let opportunity pass them by.

Another story about opportunity had its beginning in a city in western Texas. An elderly gentleman had been earning a meager living from a grocery business for more than thirty-five years, and had reached retirement age. Because of an inadequate retirement income, he was forced to enter life insurance selling as a new career at age sixty-five. He was an immediate success and qualified for the Million Dollar Round Table, which is the industry's premier award. He repeatedly told me of the tremendous fulfillment and happiness that he was receiving from his work. His annual income was considerably more during retirement than during his peak earning years in the grocery business. He said that he wished with all his heart that this opportunity had been available in his youth, so that he could have become financially independent. I don't believe he ever stopped to realize that this opportunity had been available when he was younger, but he had not taken time to discover it. It is never too late to start living a happy and successful life, but the sooner you begin, the greater the results.

It was Francis Bacon, English philosopher, essayist, and statesman, who wrote, "A wise man will make more opportunities than he finds." Don't be so idealistic as to think that someone is going to give you an opportunity that will make you rich and successful. People tend to keep those kinds of opportunities for themselves. Yes, you must make your opportunities just as Francis Bacon said, that is, if you want to enjoy the happy and successful life.

God has provided everything you need to live the good life. You are exposed to exciting new opportunities each day. To capitalize on them, you must grasp only those opportunities that are in harmony with your ability to take advantage of them.

You possess the spirit within you to be happy and successful, and now you have learned you live in a world which provides you with unlimited opportunity. When you really think about it—you've got everything goin' for you!

Remember the Apostle Paul's words, "Don't copy the behavior and customs of this world, but be a new and different person with a fresh newness in all you do and think." Remember that you are important, that you are loved, that you are a unique creation, and that you have unlimited opportunity available because you live in a world governed by a Creator who knows no limitations. In God's world, "You can be great if you believe you can!"

Before going on to the next chapter you must accept the following principles:

1. *You can be happy and successful and that's the way the Creator wants you to live.*
2. *You live in a world that offers the opportunity and abundance to achieve all your fondest dreams.*
3. *Opportunity is everywhere, waiting to be discovered.*

Accepting these principles takes you another step closer to a life of happiness and prosperity.

Key Points to Commit to Memory

- You are important!
- Conformity destroys a man's initiative and independence.
- You can be great if you believe you can!
- Happiness and success are attitudes of mind.
- If you have worthwhile goals and are going in the right direction, all of your needs will be provided for.
- Each of us has within him the seed of greatness!
- You are loved so much that a Man gave his life for you.
- As you observe all the tremendous abundance around you, remember this, you have as much right to that abundance as any other person.
- Opportunity comes to those who seek it.
- Opportunity is everywhere!
- Fear of failure has caused many capable men to let opportunity pass them by.
- You've got everything goin' for you.

10

Time Won't Wait

If you were going to live to be seven or eight hundred, you could afford to waste three or four hundred years of your life doing unimportant things! You would still have enough time left to change your life and become happy and successful.

This is not the case! From the moment you draw your first breath, you begin a personal race against time. The normal life expectancy is approximately sixty-seven years—and that's not very long. You are running out of time!

Time is like a precious jewel. It must be guarded well and worn with discretion or you will suddenly realize that it has been stolen.

As each second, minute, hour, day, week, month, and year pass into history, they are gone forever. Time can never be replaced once it is lost! Time is your most priceless asset! How you use time determines whether you add to your wealth or remain right where you are.

If you use your time wisely and with great respect, your life will be one of abundance, but if you neglect time, it will neglect you. Each day is very important to you because you exchange one entire day of your life for it.

You have just as much time as the Rockefellers, Morgans, or Fords had when they began to build their vast fortunes. You possess as much time as Einstein did when he made his great discoveries regarding our universe. You have the same amount of time that Edison had when he invented the electric light. Each of us has as much time available as Tolstoy had when he wrote *War and Peace.* Each of us has the same amount of time as did Coach Vince Lombardi when he won three successive world championships while at the helm of the Green Bay Packers.

I recently heard the Reverend Bob Richards, a former Olympic pole vault champion, say that beginning at thirteen, he spent over 10,000 hours practicing the pole vault and that you can be good at anything if you will put over 10,000 hours of work into it. He put time to work for himself and became a world-famous athlete.

A *Reader's Digest* article revealed how Henry J. Kaiser made time add to his success. The article stated: "Henry Kaiser is one of the most time-conscious people in the world. Even the five hours he allots himself for sleep are productive. This is what he calls the 'idea period' and he always has a pad and pencil next to his bed."

The news media were fascinated by the skillful use of time and the tremendous drive and zeal that former President Lyndon B. Johnson poured into his work. He would rise promptly at 6:30 A.M. and then work until ten or eleven almost every night. Fourteen-hour work days were not rare in his life! Through the skillful use of time, he was accomplishing almost twice as much every day as the average man who works eight hours. Is it any wonder he became president or that he was such a successful businessman?

Proper use of time is one of the most important keys to leading a happy and successful life and enjoying balanced living. You must learn to worship when you worship! Work when you work! Study when you study! And play when you play!

You must allot enough time for each of the four areas of planning: spiritual, financial, educational, and recreational—then you will have balance which is most important to your happiness and success. You should be actively engaged in the pursuit of the accomplishment of your goals in these four areas of your life every waking moment.

Use your time in an organized and productive manner, and you will accomplish your goals in the business and personal areas, and still have time left for fun and fellowship with family and friends. Time control does not restrict your activities, it gives you freedom—freedom to do everything that your heart desires. The man who has plans and controls his time is the only free man. All others are slaves and conform to mediocre standards. The writer of Ecclesiastes understood that for each man under the heaven there is necessity for the proper control of time:

There is a right time for everything:
    A time to be born, a time to die;
    A time to plant, a time to harvest;
    A time to kill, a time to heal;
    A time to destroy, a time to rebuild;
    A time to cry, a time to laugh;
    A time to grieve, a time to dance;
    A time for scattering stones, a time for gathering stones;
    A time to hug, a time not to hug;
    A time to find, a time to lose;

A time for keeping, a time for throwing away;
A time to tear, a time to repair;
A time to be quiet, a time to speak up;
A time for loving, a time for hating;
A time for war, a time for peace
(Ecclesiastes 3:1-8).

You might have wasted yesterday! You may even be wasting today! But you haven't yet wasted tomorrow, for it has not yet come, and is kept fresh and waiting for you. You can turn over a new leaf with each dawning day if you choose, but remember, time is speeding away from you—so don't delay! The proper use of time in your life will guarantee your happiness and success. How do you use your tremendous gift of time?

Time is money! Do you know how much your time is worth? The chart on the following page shows how valuable your time really is.

Isn't it amazing just how much one extra hour's work each day can mean to you over a period of thirty years?

You can earn a fortune if you will take advantage of time and are willing to pay the price of hard work. Nothing worthwhile may be accomplished without it. The successful man learns to work from "can to can't." He must put aside the eight-to-five concept. He must develop a work-until-the-job-is-completed attitude. He must learn to do whatever is necessary to accomplish the task before him. He must put the job before the hours. He must be goal-oriented. He must learn to drive himself until work has become a habit that is stronger than his human desire to loaf. A wise proverb tells us: "Lazy men are soon poor; hard workers get rich" (Proverbs 10:4).

We live in an age of gross materialism. Increasing

THE VALUE OF YOUR TIME
IN DOLLARS AND CENTS
EIGHT HOUR WORK DAY
244 WORK DAYS PER YEAR

Annual income	Each minute worth	Each hour worth	One hour per day for one year is worth	One hour per day for thirty years is worth
$ 5,000	$ .0426	$ 2.56	$ 625	$ 18,750
6,000	.0531	3.07	750	22,500
7,000	.0598	3.59	875	26,250
8,000	.0683	4.10	1,000	30,000
10,000	.0852	5.12	1,250	37,500
12,000	.1025	6.15	1,500	45,000
14,000	.1195	7.17	1,750	52,500
16,000	.1366	8.20	2,000	60,000
20,000	.1708	10.25	2,500	75,000
25,000	.2135	12.81	3,125	93,750
30,000	.2561	15.37	3,750	112,500
35,000	.2988	17.93	4,375	131,250
40,000	.3415	20.49	5,000	150,000
50,000	.4269	25.61	6,250	187,500
75,000	.6403	38.42	9,375	281,250
100,000	.8523	51.23	12,500	375,000

physical wealth is accompanied by a decline in spiritual values. There is a feeling that something is wrong. People express a feeling of emptiness and unrest. They want a four-day work week! They want more leisure time! They want to work less and play more! We are on a collision course with failure.

Although we have more leisure time than ever before, few use this time to advantage. Even so, many want even more and already in some areas four-day weeks are beginning.

If you are average, you have 2,229 hours of leisure annually—more time than the average amount of time you put in on your job.

This is the picture of the opportunity on your doorstep. Because so many are interested in getting more and more money for doing less and less, think how great the opportunity for someone who is interested in:

- Giving more and better service to the people he serves.
- Spending his time and energy in equipping himself to do a better job.
- Learning to enjoy life fully as a thoroughly "balanced" individual.
- Adding to his share of happiness.

Benjamin Franklin said, "Many a man thinks he is buying pleasure, when he is really selling himself to it."

Man rarely stops his mad rush for materialism long enough to consider the consequences! The unending source of eternal wisdom tells us:

I walked by the field of a certain lazy fellow and saw that it was overgrown with thorns, and covered with weeds; and its walls were broken down. Then, as I looked, I learned this lesson:

"A little extra sleep,

A little more slumber,

A little folding of the hands to rest"

means that poverty will break in upon you suddenly like a robber, and violently like a bandit (Proverbs 24:30-34).

Leisure time—wrongly spent—has been the downfall of great nations, as well as individuals. Aristotle, in his *Politics*, told how the proud and powerful Spartans "remained secure as long as they were at war" and then "collapsed as soon as they acquired an empire. They did not know how to use the leisure that peace brought."

A friend of mine is in the restaurant business. He has built at least ten successful restaurants each of which failed soon after they reached their peak.

Bill knew the restaurant business from pot-washing on up. He could cook; he could design a comfortable eating place to fit almost any vacant situation; and it made no difference where there was a gap in the restaurant business, he could fill it. His restaurant, whether it was Southern-style or Italian, steak and chops or seafood, was tops in town.

After each failure, Bill demonstrated that ability we all must have—he got up and began getting started all over again. He learned that valuable trait, but he never learned how to handle success.

Each new restaurant found Bill at the job at first light. He bought the freshest produce, the finest meat at the early morning markets. He supervised everything from the kitchen to the front door. He was rough on his help, but he knew how to build a good-tipping business.

He wouldn't continue to fail if he could do just one thing—learn to spend a little more time on the business once it gets under way. Bill knows when his restaurant is catching on. You can tell, too. You'll see Bill on the street, out in front of the restaurant, smoking a big cigar, or tooling his Cadillac around town. When Bill's genius disappears from the market, the kitchen, and the cash register—when he starts spending his leisure and his money away from the business, trouble sets in, and soon Bill is looking for a new location and the credit to get started again. One day, he will be old, flat broke, without credit.

Nation after nation down through history has fallen victim to idleness. The Romans worked hard at building a very affluent society but after conquering the world, they grew soft and lazy. Rome, under Nero, celebrated 176 legal holidays each year—almost one out of every two days was a time of leisure. They fell!

Many people who think they are farming in this country are mistaken. True, they spend six days, many of them long and arduous, tilling the soil, but they have scarcely begun to farm by Oriental standards.

The millions of Chinese nourish every seedling in tiny farm plots and extract far more from them than Americans would get from the same area. Tender, loving care—without regard for hours or holidays or coffee breaks—keeps these peasants from starving.

Uncontrolled materialism has extinguished the flame of many outstanding civilizations. First, they became wealthy, then weak, next apathetic, and in the end, they died!

Perhaps you know of a family business in which "shirtsleeves to shirtsleeves in three generations" has been demonstrated. Grandad has an idea and the drive and creates a substantial business. His son inherits and rides the wave of success that was built for him. During his generation, little is done to advance the business and often a bad decision or two creates problems. The grandson, educated at the best schools, unskilled in business matters, either takes full charge and runs the business into the ground or lets inefficient management do it while he enjoys his leisure.

Nations and businesses differ little from individuals. Avoid materialism and don't rest on your laurels once they are won. The parallels between the fallen civilizations and America are startling. The individual citizen in those vanished civilizations did not believe it would happen to him and his nation. It need not happen to you and your nation. To be happy and successful and continue prosperous, each of us must engage in worthwhile work and efficiently use our time. We can do this by having personal goals and plans!

America need not disappear as did the great societies of the past, but saving it will be up to each of us. Attitudes must change! We must go back to the basic principles of God and country, and again, learn to get pleasure out of work. The Creator said, "Six days shalt thou labor and do all thy work." Only when we follow this guidance will we be happy.

By making a total commitment to your work, you will be able to fully enjoy those precious days that are reserved for leisure. That commitment must be based not on temporary materialism, but on something much bigger and more worthwhile. This will give the spirit within you the opportunity to manifest itself in every area of your life.

Put your eyes on life's higher goals! And remember the old saying, "The harder you work, the luckier you get."

In Ecclesiastes 11:4, we find another of the most important keys to becoming happy and successful: "If you wait for perfect conditions, you will never get anything done." Many people wait out their lives for the perfect circumstances, so that they may enter into their life's work. Perfect circumstances will never come! Get on with your opportunity! Now is the right time! Act!

Many people resemble the little-known painter who planned to paint a masterpiece. He described it in detail to his friends many times as the years passed, but he never found the right time and conditions to begin painting. Time sped by and he became old and sick. He took his masterpiece to his grave with him, for it lived only within the spirit inside of him. Had he acted when he first conceived the idea, it would have become a reality and would have lived on and on, benefiting future generations.

Don't reach the sunset of life having accomplished nothing worthwhile. Can you imagine the discouragement of looking back at your life and seeing nothing but a void? Forget about your age, status, nationality, or color—decide what you really want from life—then go after it—you are never too old or too young to begin. Action makes dreams become reality. There are millions and millions of good ideas in this world and the man who takes one of them and puts it into practice is priceless. You can be that man, if you believe you can!

The vital elements of the happy and successful life are: time, work, and action! Time control combined with hard work and action built on the firm foundation of belief creates a potent force.

Before going on to the next chapter you must accept the following principle:

"Time control combined with hard work and action and built on the firm foundation of belief are the vital elements of the happy and successful life. You must be willing to pay the price!"

Accepting this principle takes you another step closer to achieving your fondest dreams.

Key Points to Commit to Memory

- Time is your most valuable asset.
- Each day is important to you because it is a segment of your life, and once past, it can never be regained.
- The man who plans and controls his time is the only free man.
- Time is money!
- Nothing worthwhile may be accomplished without hard work.
- You must learn to drive yourself until work has become a habit that is stronger than your human desire to loaf.
- The harder you work, the luckier you get!
- Get on with your opportunity!
- Action makes dreams become reality!

The Way
Is Given

The line has been drawn! See it, it is right there on the ground before you. If you step over it, you will have inner peace, riches, enlightenment, and physical well-being. Taking that step means that you unconditionally accept the principles brought forth within these pages. It also means that you must put them to work in your life today. Now is the time to decide to take that step—go ahead—take it! Wonderful! You made it!

Now that you have crossed over the line and as you begin to live this happy and successful way, you will find that the flood gates of balanced living will open and pour over you more happiness and success than you ever dreamed existed. Your success may include money. But even more important, you will have experienced inner peace greater than ever before. Your view of your opportunities and the future will be overwhelming and you will feel better than you have in many years. You will be among a very exclusive minority who lead wonderfully happy and successful lives. Begin today! You really have nothing to lose, but you do have a happy and successful life to gain!

There is an ancient legend about a time in the

history of mankind when society so abused Wisdom that the Wisemen decided to take the secret of happiness and success away from man and hide it where he would never again find it. The big question was—where should they hide it?

A council was called by the Chief of the Wisemen to discuss this question. The lesser of the Wisemen said, "We will bury the secret of happiness and success deep in the earth."

But the Chief of the Wisemen said, "No, that will never do, for man will dig deep down into the earth and find it."

Then they said, "Well, we will sink the secret of happiness and success into the dark depths of the deepest ocean."

But again the Chief Wiseman replied, "No, not there, for man will learn to dive into the deep dark depths of the ocean and will find it."

Then one of the lesser Wisemen said, "We will take it to the top of the highest mountain and hide it there."

But again, the Chief Wiseman replied, "No, for man will eventually climb even the highest of mountains and find it, and again take it up for himself."

Then the lesser of the Wisemen decided to give up and concluded, "We do not know where it can be hidden. It seems that there is no place on the earth or in the sea that man will not eventually discover."

Then the Chief Wiseman said, "Here is what we will do with the secret of happiness and success. We will hide it deep inside of man himself, for he will never think to look for it there."

To this day, according to the legend, man has been running to and fro over the earth—digging—diving—and climbing, searching for something that he already possesses within himself.

Almost two thousand years ago, Jesus showed us how to find this secret. Let his life be the example by which you will achieve happiness and success and you cannot possibly fail!

Between the covers of this book, I have put it all together for you—complete—concise—and to the point! There is no theory here, only sound principles based on natural laws. I *know* they work, for I have tasted fire and seen the rain, but I have also seen the sunshine! Now, I pass this wisdom on to you, my only motive being to help you.

May the Creator bless you as he has me.

Part 2

Your Plan
of Action

How to Make Your Own Plan of Action

The Beginning

The Plan of Action is the heart of the Bland Method of Goal Setting and Planning program. It is the tool responsible for converting thought into action. Without a Plan of Action your goals would be meaningless and worthless. It may take days, months or even years for you to develop the perfect Plan of Action for your life, so do not be discouraged if you cannot work out every minute detail in the beginning. All of the minute details will come to you in time. The important thing is to start now, even if you must begin on a very short-range basis. As you experience personal growth, it will be necessary to revise your Plan of Action periodically in order to keep it up to date and challenging. Remember to keep your Plan of Action before you each day. If you do, your goals will become a reality in your life.

Recommended Procedure

Do not attempt to fill out your Plan of Action until you possess a basic understanding of the principles already discussed in Part 1. You may want to look through the entire program just to familiarize yourself with its contents, but if you want to receive its full benefits please apply the following procedure:

- First, familiarize yourself with the entire Bland Method of Goal Setting and Planning program.
- Second, read and reread the material until it is understood.
- Third, complete the Plan of Action, following the instructions very closely.
- Fourth, undertake a systematic reading program, using the Bibliography of Suggested Reading at the end of this book.

Completing the Plan of Action

After you sincerely feel that you thoroughly understand the principles, you are then ready to begin filling out your Plan of Action. Completing the Plan of Action necessitates being very specific regarding your own personal goals. You must set aside some uninterrupted time when you can devote all of your concentration and effort to working on the plan. Your Plan of Action should include detailed goals and plans for both you and your family—they cannot be separated. When completing the plan, you should commit yourself to the following:

- One, be perfectly honest with yourself.
- Two, dare to think big.
- Three, take action.
- Four, believe in your plan.

Your Personal Affirmation

Write out a detailed description of the person you want to become. Consider the four areas of personal planning: What kind of person do you want to become spiritually? What kind of person do you want to become financially? What kind of person do you want to become educationally? What kind of person do you want to become recreationally?

Crystallize your thinking in each of the preceding areas. Be very specific! Great care should be given to writing the description of the person you want to become because you will become that person! *This affirmation should be read each morning during your Faith Period.* This procedure will program your subconscious mind to take up the role of this new person. Don't forget, reading this affirmation daily is a must! Things to consider when completing your personal affirmation:

- How can you achieve peace of mind?
- What sort of work will you do?
- How much do you want to earn?
- What kind of home will you live in?
- How will you dress?
- What kind of automobile will you drive?
- What will others think of you?
- How will you help others?
- Will you be knowledgeable?
- What will you do for pleasure?
- Will you be balanced?
- Will you become wise?

What Is Your Present Situation?

You must determine where you presently are, before you can establish sound plans to determine where you are going. You must analyze each of the four areas of personal planning in detail. Determine if your present situation is satisfactory or unsatisfactory. Then commit it to writing by checking one of the boxes and describing your present situation in detail, be it positive or negative. Simply take an honest look at yourself and write it down. Once you display the courage to admit the sort of person you really are, you will be well on your way to self-improvement. Things to consider when analyzing your present situation in each of the four planning areas:

- Is my present situation satisfactory or unsatisfactory?
- What makes my present situation satisfactory?
- What makes my present situation unsatisfactory?
- How can I change my present situation?
- Do I lead a balanced life?
- Do I want to change my present situation?
- Am I straightforward and honest with myself?

Short-range and Long-range Goal Setting

Each of the four areas of personal planning are separated into three divisions: One-Year Goals—Five-Year Goals—and Ultimate Goals. Through these three divisions you find both short-range and long-range goal setting. If you experience a difficult time when attempting to plan on a long-range basis, you may be better off if you complete only the short-range goals. Don't concern yourself if your goals are not elaborate in the beginning. That will come with time. Now, let's discuss the three divisions of goal setting:

1. One-Year Goals—This is short-range goal setting. These goals should be established on a calendar-year basis. Set your goals to be accomplished during the remainder of the current year. These goals are very important, due to the fact that they

are short-range and give you the opportunity to experience immediate results. Be very specific when setting one-year goals.

2. Five-Year Goals—These are classified as intermediate-range goals. These goals should be established based on current projections of your future potential. These goals should be adjusted and updated every year so that they will remain in line with your personal growth. Decide where you want to be five years from now and then commit it to writing.

3. Ultimate Goals—These are long-range goals, lifetime goals. The target date for their completion may be established at a certain age or in a specific number of years—it's up to you. In the beginning, you may find it very difficult to establish long-range goals. If you do, stick with short-range and intermediate-range planning. Your long-range plans will reveal themselves to you when you have made yourself ready to receive them. Project yourself on out to age sixty-five, seventy, or seventy-five and give serious thought as to what kind of life you will want then. Also, think about all of the things you would like to accomplish during your lifetime.

Your Spiritual Goals

Keeping in mind your personal affirmation and the analysis of your present situation, it is time to begin to set goals in the spiritual realm of your life. Man by his very nature possesses an innate desire to worship and he is not happy until this innate desire is being fulfilled. The spiritual area of your plans is perhaps the most important, for it provides the belief and faith necessary for the achievement of all your goals in the other three areas of planning. Please apply the procedure outlined in Short-Range and Long-Range Goal Setting regarding the three divisions of goal setting: One-Year Goals—Five-Year Goals—and Ultimate Goals. Things to consider when you are setting your Spiritual Goals:

- Do you give to worthwhile causes?
- Where can you go to receive spiritual growth?
- Where can you go to become involved in spiritually stimulating activity?
- Is your spiritual life balanced?
- Do you include your family in your spiritual plans?
- What do you want to do to make this a better world?
- Do you read and study the Bible?
- Have you planned your Faith Period?
- Do you meditate and pray?
- Do you believe in the Creator?
- How can you make a spiritual contribution of lasting value?
- How are you going to help others?

Your Financial Goals

Keeping in mind your personal affirmation and the analysis of your present situation, you are now ready to establish your financial goals. Money is very necessary if you are to be happy and successful, but it must be kept in the proper perspective. We receive money as a reward for our services—the more service we render, the more money we receive. Please apply the procedure outlined in Short-Range and Long-Range Goal Setting regarding the three divisions of goal setting: One-Year Goals—Five-Year Goals—and Ultimate Goals.

Things to be considered when you are setting Your Financial Goals:

- How much money do you want to earn?
- How much money are you going to save?
- How much money are you going to give to worthwhile causes?
- When do you want to retire?
- How much income do you want in retirement?
- What kind of work do you really want to do?
- Do you abuse the use of charge accounts and credit cards?
- Do you have a realistic budget for your family?
- Are all of your family's financial needs adequately met?
- What will be your net worth five years from now?
- What will be your net worth at retirement?
- Do you possess financial balance in your life?

Your Educational Goals

Keeping in mind your personal affirmation and the analysis of your present situation, you are now ready to establish your goals in the educational area. Specialized knowledge will be very important as you progress toward the accomplishment of your goals. Mental growth is very necessary to great achievement. Please apply the procedure outlined in Short-Range and Long-Range Goal Setting regarding the three divisions of goal setting: One-Year Goals—Five-Year Goals—and Ultimate Goals. Things to be considered when you are setting Your Educational Goals:

- Are you helping your family to set goals and make plans?
- Are your children going to college?

- Will you quit reading literary trash?
- Will you put only wholesome information into your mind?
- Do you have a daily time for study?
- Are you going to achieve great wisdom?
- Do you know all there is to know about your work?
- Does your wife have a program to gain mental growth?
- Will you share your knowledge with others?
- Can you force yourself to become a student?
- Do you possess educational balance in your life?

Your Recreational Goals

Keeping in mind your personal affirmation and the analysis of your present situation, you are now ready to set your recreational goals. A creative, success-oriented mind cannot function in a neglected body. If you are going to pay the price of success, you must be in good physical shape to do it. Otherwise, you may suffer a heart attack or some other disease brought about by your neglect. Your body is the temple of your mind, so care for it well! Please apply the procedure outlined in Short-Range and Long-Range Goal Setting regarding the three divisions of goal setting: One-Year Goals—Five-Year Goals—and Ultimate Goals. Things to consider when you are setting Your Recreational Goals:

- Do you have a personal fitness program?
- Do you enjoy personal recreation?
- Do you plan time for family recreation?
- What was your waist size when you graduated from high school?
- Do you take vacations?
- Do you do things that provide mental relaxation?

- Do you have regularly scheduled medical check-ups?
- Have you read *The New Aerobics* by Kenneth H. Cooper, M.D.?
- Do you have fun from your personal and family recreation?
- Do you really want to be physically and mentally fit?
- Where can you become involved in worthwhile recreational programs?
- Are you living a recreationally balanced life?

Your Monthly Activity Calendar

Now that you have made your personal affirmation, analyzed your personal situation, and set goals in the four areas of personal planning, it is time to take action. You will begin by planning the most efficient use of your time on the Monthly Activity Calendar. These plans should be established on a calendar-year basis. You should begin today, and make plans for the remainder of the current year. The following procedure should be used when completing Your Monthly Activity Planner:

- Write in the names of the remaining months in the current calendar year at the top of each page.
- Write in the dates of each day of the remaining months in the small squares located in the upper left hand corner of the larger squares.
- You should now have a complete planning calendar for the remainder of the current year.
- Now, go through each month day by day and plan all of your days off for the remainder of the year. Be very honest. Do not deceive yourself! If you are not going to work, please plan it just that way. Time off

149

constitutes time that you will not be actively working at your job. Consider the following when planning your time off:

    vacations
    birthdays
    anniversaries
    recreation
    rest
    weekends
    holidays
    special occasions
    conventions and meetings
    parties

- Now that you have planned all of your time off for the remainder of the year, count the number of work days you have left to accomplish your objectives. Let nothing interfere with your planned work days. Let others plan their activities around you and your family.
- Keep your Monthly Activity Calendars up to date. Enter any new activities on the calendar as soon as they are definite.
- Count the number of off days on your Monthly Activity Calendar. Many times this is an eye opener.
- Stick with your monthly plans once they are made.
- Give copies of your monthly plans to key people to keep them informed.
- Transfer your plans from your Monthly Activity Calendar to the Weekly Activity Planner.
- Let your Monthly Activity Calendar guide all of your activity.

Your Weekly Activity Planner

Now you will become more specific with your planning process through the use of your Weekly Activity

Planner. The procedure for making definite weekly plans is as follows:

- Each week's planned activity should be taken from your Monthly Activity Calendar and transferred to your Weekly Activity Planner.
- Place the week's date at the top of the planner.
- Place your goals for the week at the top of the Planner.
- You should list a minimum of ten top priority items to be accomplished in any given week.
- All activity in the four areas of your personal goals should be included on your Weekly Activity Planner.
- Keep your Weekly Activity Planner in a place where it may readily be seen at all times.
- Any top priority items that are not accomplished in a given week should be carried over to the following week for their fulfillment.
- Your Weekly Activity Planner should be filled out during your Faith Period at the end of each week for the purpose of planning the next week's activity. Always plan at least one week in advance.
- Keep your Weekly Activity Planners so that they may be analyzed at the end of the calendar year to aid in helping you establish new plans.
- The Weekly Activity Planner is a separate book of fifty-two pages which may be ordered by writing Bland Institute, 7145 Chevy Chase, Memphis, Tennessee 38115. It is strongly recommended that you order this planner. It is a must when executing your plan of action.

Your Daily Activity Planner

The final step in the planning process is the Daily Activity Planner. This is the most important part of the planning process since this is your detailed action planner. It goes with you everywhere you go—guiding your destiny. You must use a Daily Activity Planner if you are to efficiently execute your Plan of Action. The procedure for using your Daily Activity Planner is as follows:

- Each day's planned activity should be taken from your Weekly Activity Planner and transferred to your Daily Activity Planner.
- You should set aside some time during your Faith Period each morning to review your Weekly Activity Planner and fill out your Daily Activity Planner.
- Place the day's date at the top of the planner.
- Write out your goals for the day.
- List the day's top priority items.
- Be very specific concerning information that is placed on the Daily Activity Planner—names, places, times, dates.
- Include all activity on the Daily Activity Planner, even things as minor as "getting your hair groomed." Also all spiritual, financial, educational, and recreational plans.
- Take the list of ten priority items from your Weekly Activity Planner and divide them up by day for their accomplishment.
- Include any special notes acquired during the day on the back of the Daily Activity Planner— names to remember—telephone numbers— business expenses—etc.
- At the end of the day, take time to list your results on the back of the Daily Activity Planner. This will provide you a realistic look at your day's activity.
- Write your favorite success prompter on the back of the Daily Activity Planner. Refer to it when strength is needed to carry on with the day's task.

Everyone has favorite motivational sayings that mean a great deal to them—so write yours on your daily planner.

- You should carry a copy of your Daily Activity Planner with you for quick reference at all times during the day.
- Check off items from your Daily Activity Planner as they are accomplished.
- Keep your Daily Activity Planners so that they may be analyzed at the end of the calendar year when new plans are being made. The Daily Activity Planners can be ordered by writing the Bland Institute, 7145 Chevy Chase, Memphis, Tennessee 38115. These planners will force you to be successful if you will use them.

Your Faith Card

You may want to carry a Faith Card with you each day to give you added strength in time of need. The Faith Card should be completed as follows:

- List your major goals in your four planning areas.
- Write the price you are willing to pay to accomplish these goals.
- List the things you are thankful for.
- List your latest great accomplishment.
- List your favorite success prompter.
- Complete your Faith Card expressing your own personal interest.
- Read your Faith Card three times each day—morning, noon, and night. This procedure will program your subconscious mind.
- Make a Faith Card for each month of the year—carry it with you at all times—it will give you courage when needed.

- Faith Cards may be ordered by writing The Bland Institute.

Your Visualization Board

"If you keep your goal constantly before you each day, it is certain to become a reality."

- A simple and effective means of keeping your goal before you is by using a Visualization Board.
- Purchase a large sheet of poster paper and then glue pictures of your goals onto the poster.
- Place it where it can be seen several times each day.
- Color pictures for the Visualization Board may be found in books, magazines, etc.
- Through the use of the Visualization Board your goals are indelibly engraved on your subconscious. This is just another method of keeping your goals before you.

Your Success Prompter

Write your favorite motivation sayings on posters, cards, etc. and place them in locations where they will be constantly seen each day. They will give you much needed inspiration.

MY PERSONAL AFFIRMATION REGARDING THE PERSON I WANT TO BECOME

_____

_____

_____

_____

_____

_____

_____

_____

_____

_____

_____

_____

_____

_____

_____

_____

WHAT IS MY PRESENT SITUATION?

Spiritual   Satisfactory   Unsatisfactory

_____

_____

_____

_____

Financial   Satisfactory   Unsatisfactory

_____

_____

_____

Educational   Satisfactory   Unsatisfactory

_____

_____

_____

Recreational   Satisfactory   Unsatisfactory

_____

_____

_____

_____

MY SPIRITUAL GOALS

One-Year Goals
_____

_____

_____

_____

_____

_____

Five-Year Goals
_____

_____

_____

_____

_____

Ultimate Goals
_____

By Age _____ Or In Years _____

_____

_____

_____

_____

_____

MY FINANCIAL GOALS

<u>One-Year Goals</u>

_____

_____

_____

_____

_____

_____

<u>Five-Year Goals</u>

_____

_____

_____

_____

_____

_____

<u>Ultimate Goals</u>

By Age _____ Or In Years _____

_____

_____

_____

_____

_____

MY EDUCATIONAL GOALS

One-Year Goals

_____

_____

_____

_____

_____

_____

Five-Year Goals

_____

_____

_____

_____

_____

Ultimate Goals

By Age _____ Or In Years _____

_____

_____

_____

_____

_____

MY RECREATIONAL GOALS

One-Year Goals

_____

_____

_____

_____

_____

Five-Year Goals

_____

_____

_____

_____

_____

Ultimate Goals

By Age _____ Or In Years _____

_____

_____

_____

_____

_____

MY MONTHLY ACTIVITY CALENDAR

JANUARY

Sunday	Monday	Tuesday	Wednesday	Thursday	Friday	Saturday

MY MONTHLY ACTIVITY CALENDAR

FEBRUARY

Sunday	Monday	Tuesday	Wednesday	Thursday	Friday	Saturday

MY MONTHLY ACTIVITY CALENDAR

MARCH

Sunday	Monday	Tuesday	Wednesday	Thursday	Friday	Saturday

MY MONTHLY ACTIVITY CALENDAR

APRIL

Sunday	Monday	Tuesday	Wednesday	Thursday	Friday	Saturday

MY MONTHLY ACTIVITY CALENDAR

MAY

Sunday	Monday	Tuesday	Wednesday	Thursday	Friday	Saturday

MY MONTHLY ACTIVITY CALENDAR

JUNE

Sunday	Monday	Tuesday	Wednesday	Thursday	Friday	Saturday

MY MONTHLY ACTIVITY CALENDAR

JULY

Sunday	Monday	Tuesday	Wednesday	Thursday	Friday	Saturday

MY MONTHLY ACTIVITY CALENDAR

AUGUST

Sunday	Monday	Tuesday	Wednesday	Thursday	Friday	Saturday

MY MONTHLY ACTIVITY CALENDAR

SEPTEMBER

Sunday	Monday	Tuesday	Wednesday	Thursday	Friday	Saturday

MY MONTHLY ACTIVITY CALENDAR

OCTOBER

Sunday	Monday	Tuesday	Wednesday	Thursday	Friday	Saturday

MY MONTHLY ACTIVITY CALENDAR

NOVEMBER

Sunday	Monday	Tuesday	Wednesday	Thursday	Friday	Saturday

MY MONTHLY ACTIVITY CALENDAR

DECEMBER

Sunday	Monday	Tuesday	Wednesday	Thursday	Friday	Saturday

Bibliography of Suggested Reading

Read one book each month for twenty-four consecutive months as your personal program for planned enlightenment:

1. Allen, James. *As a Man Thinketh.* Old Tappan, N.J.: Fleming H. Revell, n.d.
2. Schwartz, David J. *The Magic of Thinking Big.* Englewood Cliffs, N.J.: Prentice-Hall, 1959.
3. Bristol, Claude M. *The Magic of Believing.* New York: Cornerstone, 1967.
4. Mandino, Og. *The Greatest Salesman in the World.* New York: Bantam, 1974.
5. Carnegie, Dale. *How to Win Friends and Influence People.* New York: Simon & Schuster, 1936.
6. Conwell, Russell H. *Acres of Diamonds.* New York: Harper & Row, 1915.
7. Maltz, Maxwell. *Psycho-Cybernetics.* New York: Pocket Books, 1970.
8. Schuller, Robert H. *Move Ahead with Possibility Thinking.* Old Tappan, N.J.: Fleming H. Revell, 1973.

9. Hill, Napoleon. *Think and Grow Rich*. Greenwich, Conn.: Fawcett Publications, Inc., 1976.

10. Clason, George S. *The Richest Man in Babylon*. New York: Hawthorn, 1955.

11. Steere, Daniel C. *I am—I Can*. Old Tappan, N.J.: Fleming H. Revell, 1973.

12. *Who Is This Man Jesus?* Edited by Kenneth N. Taylor, Wheaton, Ill.: Tyndale House, 1967.

13. Maltz, Maxwell. *The Magic Power of Self Image Psychology*. Englewood Cliffs, N.J.: Prentice-Hall, 1964.

14. Schuller, Robert H. *Self-love: The Dynamic Force of Success*. New York: Hawthorn, 1969.

15. Brande, Dorothea. *Wake Up and Live*. New York: Cornerstone, 1974.

16. Allen, Charles L. *God's Psychiatry*. Old Tappan, N.J.: Fleming H. Revell, 1953.

17. Hill, Napoleon. *Grow Rich with Peace of Mind*. New York: Hawthorn, 1967.

18. Otis, George. *God, Money and You*. Van Nuys, Calif.: Bible Voice, 1975.

19. Wright, Norman. *Improving Your Self-image*. Irvine, Calif.: Harvest House, 1977.

20. Jones, Charlie. *Life is Tremendous*. Wheaton, Ill.: Tyndale House, 1968.

21. Fromm, Erich. *The Art of Loving*. New York: Harper & Row, 1962.

22. Bloodworth, Venice. *Key to Yourself*. Los Angeles: Scrivener & Co., 1975.

23. DeVos, Richard M. *Believe!* Old Tappan, N.J.: Fleming H. Revell, 1975.

24. *The Living Bible*. Wheaton, Ill.: Tyndale House, 1971. (I highly recommend the self-help edition.) The happy and successful individual should read and study this book for the remainder of life!

If you have questions about how to become a Christian, you are cordially invited to write for a helpful booklet that will be sent to you free of charge.

Address your request to:
The Bland Institute
P.O. Box 40082
Memphis, Tennessee 38104

I do not choose to be a common man.
It is my right to be uncommon—
   if I can.
I seek opportunity, not security.
I do not wish to be a kept citizen,
   humbled and dulled by having the
   state look after me.
I want to take the calculated risk,
   to dream and to build, to fail and
   to succeed.
I refuse to barter incentive for a dole.
I prefer the challenges of life to a
   guaranteed existence, the thrill of
   fulfillment to the stale calm of Utopia.
I will not trade freedom for beneficence,
   nor dignity for a handout.
It is my heritage to think and to act
   for myself, enjoy the benefit of my
   creations, and to face the world
   boldly and say, "With God's help,
   this I have done."